39
59
62
86
96

Columbia University Lectures

PRESENT DAY JAPAN

JULIUS BEER FOUNDATION

1924

PRESENT DAY JAPAN

BY
YUSUKE TSURUMI

Special Edition Printed for the
JAPAN SOCIETY
36 WEST 44TH STREET
NEW YORK CITY

NEW YORK
COLUMBIA UNIVERSITY PRESS

CONTENTS

PRESENT DAY JAPAN

LECTURE I

THE OLD ORDER

THE honor of an invitation to lecture in this great university is one which every Japanese student may well covet. In all the colleges and universities of Japan the works of Columbia professors are read and respected as authorities of the first rank. In every branch of public service and private enterprise throughout the Japanese Empire are to be found Japanese graduates of this institution. When we cross the narrow seas to China we find Columbia graduates among the leaders in every sphere of culture also in that ancient and charming nation. Tokyo has its Columbia Club which holds periodical meetings and gives the right hand of fellowship to Columbia graduates who visit the land of the Rising Sun. As I read of the rapid expansion of this university under the able direction of President Butler, I am led to wonder whether our Japanese institutions of higher learning may not be absorbed in the extension department of Columbia in the near future!

The spirit of this university, as I understand it, is the spirit of challenging directness and scientific inquiry. So I feel under obligation to give you frankly

at the very outset the burden of my argument which
is to be sustained in detail by my series of lectures.
It is that changes of epochal significance have taken
place in the Orient during the past four of five years
— changes which render obsolete the historical treatises now used in the schools — changes which aug-
ment the weight of the East in world affairs — changes
which concern above all the United States and Japan
as Pacific powers. The dikes of the unchanging East
have burst, and the floods run under the bridge so
swiftly that the old observers are breathless; and those
who formed their judgments on the state of things
yesterday must revise their opinions to-day. A new
Asia confronts us.

Only a few years ago the powers of the world treated
China as an entity, a body politic, ruled by a sovereign authority with its center at Peking; the hypothe-
sis was always more or less tenuous, and the policies
founded upon it never worked with precision. To-
day, even this fiction is abandoned and all mankind
waits on the conflict of social forces in China — a conflict that may last a thousand years as in the feudal
Europe that followed the collapse of Rome, or that
may be resolved before we are aware by some stroke
of state foreseen only by the gods of fate. In India,
where British rule seemed secure for centuries to come,
a new spirit, a wide-spread unrest, challenges the old
order — with what hazardous consequences no living
person can divine. And where is the great Muscovite
Empire that thundered now at the gates of the Baltic,
now at the straits, now at the Far Pacific? The rivalry
of powers in Siberia that vexed the capitals of ten

countries a few months ago has been resolved by the
extension of Soviet authority over that vast region.
Moscow and Peking have begun to gather up the
threads of their diplomacy; the silence of the Russian
Embassy in the legation compound is broken by the
feverish activities of shrewd men whose profession is
revolution and whose astuteness is not to be denied.
And last but not least, Japan is being subjected to
changes so deep and thoroughgoing that a new era no
less remarkable and critical than the Restoration of
1868 is now upon us. There, of course, the old landmarks have not been submerged, and superficial observers imagine that as it was yesterday, it shall be
forever; but in fact Japan also bows to the universal
law of change. Shifting economic forces, the cumula-
tive clangor of the printing press, the steady drive of
universal education, the repercussion of changes in foreign countries, and the growing pressure of interests
in the Pacific — all these things are working out a new
social and political pattern in Japan.

It is not given to mortal men to see over the horizon
of to-morrow, but can we doubt that the flooding and
ebbing tides of the East will beat along the shores
of the West? The late President Roosevelt, as you
know, was fond of saying that ancient civilization
flourished on the Mediterranean with Rome as the
strategic center, that modern civilization has grown
upon the Atlantic, and that the future belongs to the
Pacific. There seems to be solid substance in that
contention. The vast Pacific, seventy times the area
of the Mediterranean, nearly twice the area of the Atlantic, stretches under every clime and washes the

shores of vast continents inhabited by peoples of every race and in every stage of social development. Civilizations old and new, endowed with vast resources and immense commercial strength, border upon it. Fast steamers can plow their way from Seattle to Yokohama in less time than it took a Roman captain to sail from Gibraltar to Phoenicia, — in one-fourth the time consumed by the clipper of Washington's day in crossing the Atlantic. The islands of the United States stretching off the coast of Alaska are only seven hundred miles from the boundaries of Japan; they are not so far from Japan as Chicago is from New York; swift airplanes can make the journey in a few hours in the trail of the recent path breakers. That is not all. On a clear day the last Formosan outpost of the Japanese Empire can be seen with a glass from the nearest island of the Philippine group. America's trade is bound to expand in the East; America's intellectual interest is destined to reach out more and more to Asia; the achievements of America in science, commerce, and diplomacy will weigh heavily in the Pacific balance. The policies, ideals, and measures of America, therefore, have a deeper significance for Japan than those of all the other nations on the globe combined.

And what shall we say of Japan? Is it immodest to declare that she occupies a strategic position on the western shores of the Pacific? Mr. Hughes may announce the end of the Lansing-Ishii agreement; the geographical and economic facts underlying it remain unchanged. At all events, it cannot be denied that Japan must sit at every council table where the affairs of the Orient are discussed and adjusted. Her policies.

ideals, and measures must in turn inevitably affect America, not so deeply of course, but still vitally.

Though this is true, I do not find any responsible statesman in Japan who believes that any issue arising between the two nations cannot be solved by methods of conciliation and compromise. I am sure that not one views the possibility of war with America in any other light than that of horror. On the contrary they are grateful to the United States for innumerable services rendered since the opening of our gates by Admiral Perry, and they believe that the fundamental purposes of the American people are pacific. Yet they are admittedly puzzled by the numerous statements of high American authorities implying that our relations must be strained and that the imminence of war must always be uppermost in our minds. For example, last June, Rear Admiral Bradley A. Fiske, in a public statement to the Secretary of the Navy, warned the United States against too much confidence in pacific relations with Japan. "I do not mean to suggest," he said, "that war is even possible; but nevertheless, it may be pointed out that the Japanese and the Americans have taken attitudes that are irreconcilable, and that the Japanese have virtually broken off diplomatic relations by giving their ambassador a 'vacation'! Such attitudes and such acts have usually preceded wars though they have not always been followed by wars. But even if war is not to come, the American people ought to realize that we are unprepared for it if it does come." Then again, only three weeks ago, Mr. Wilbur, the Secretary of the Navy, standing on the shores of the Pacific, said, in words of painfully obvious implication, "There is nothing so cooling to a hot temper as a piece of cold steel."

I do not utter a breath of criticism against these high authorities for the sentiments they have expressed. It would be wholly improper for me to do so in this forum. On reading these words, however, I am profoundly pained to learn that Americans of such undoubted position and character regard my country as a standing menace to the security of the United States, and I am driven to wonder whether these opinions represent the solemn judgment of the American people. If they do, then there must be a new searching of hearts in Japan.

Is it really inevitable that the two countries should glower at each other across the Pacific as did Rome and Carthage across the Mediterranean? Frankly I do not believe that this must be. Openly and without reserve, I declare my opinion that a war between the United States and Japan would be stupid, profitless, and calamitous beyond measure, no matter what the result might be. By no conceivable calculation could either country gather from such a disaster fruits of any value comparable to the cost in life and treasure and human anguish. It is understanding, conciliation, and negotiation that we need; not bickering, controversy and defiance. Therefore, a part of my argument — the justification of these lectures — is that American scholars, publicists, and journalists should give more attention than ever to the current tendencies in Japanese life. A distinguished trustee of this University established in the Imperial University of Tokyo a chair in American history and institutions.

It is too much to hope that a similar chair in Japanese history and institutions may be sometime founded in Columbia University — here in the very center of American intellectual and economic power?

It will be my purpose in these lectures to develop the argument that I have presented in this introduction and to show, if my powers permit, that the study of Japanese history and institutions is worthy of your labors and your talents — American labors and talents bestowed with such unremitting zeal on the history and institutions of Europe. It is my intention to discuss, in such detail as time will permit, the clash of interests and classes in Japan, the tendencies in current opinion, the influences of these forces on foreign policies, and, what is of vital importance to friends of peace, the influence of foreign relations upon the course of Japanese domestic affairs. After all, the drama of politics in Japan is not altogether novel; the names, the language, the theater, are strange to most Occidentals; but the plot is as old as Euripides. There are forces that work for the dominance of statesmen who believe in what are called, in the polite language of diplomacy, " vigorous foreign policies "; even the late Mr. Lodge would hardly take that as a " veiled threat." There are forces that work for the dominance of statesmen who would direct the energies of the nation mainly to the solution of pressing internal questions; and who would pursue, in the sphere of foreign relations, the policy of conciliation, coöperation, and peace. There are in spirit Disraelis and Morleys in Japan. The things that are said and done in the homes, lecture rooms, and council chambers of America will pro-

foundly affect the fortunes of politics in Japan, and
the politics of Japan will no doubt affect in turn the
drift of events throughout the world. For this we
have the high authority of the late President Roosevelt, who saw clearly that the East and the West,
though twain, were forever one, in the strife and inter-
course of nations. To give the first chapter in the
Japanese story will be the purpose of this lecture.

If I may be allowed to anticipate, I will venture
to say again that throughout this story from the beginning to the latest cable, the United States of America
has played an important rôle in our development —
one that is destined to be even more impressive in
the future.

Japan is intensely eager to know and understand
America. Our newspapers and magazines are constantly publishing articles about this great country,
while new books about America and Americans are
published by the dozen every month.

Never before has American influence in Japan been
so great as it is to-day. In almost every Tokyo street
you may read the unmistakable signs. Things American are everywhere. In the business center of Tokyo
stand huge office buildings of distinctly American de-
sign, and you might be made homesick by the sight
of so many Ford automobiles parked at the curb.

American influence is still more noticeable in our
homes, where we have adopted all the conveniences
and comforts of American life — from Victor phono-
graphs to ice cream freezers. American motion pictures have become one of the principal amusements
of the Japanese people, and although all kissing scenes

have been deleted by the police board in the past, I understand there is now a new rule which tolerates movie kisses lasting no longer than thirty seconds!

English is spoken throughout Japan, and to some extent, what your Mr. H. L. Mencken calls the "American language"; but we have improved somewhat on your grammar and pronunciation — to the great dismay of visiting Americans.

I might continue indefinitely enumerating such illustrations of the Americanization of Japan. My only regret is that we are not able to Japanize you Americans, to even the score. The great westward drive of your civilization has crossed the American prairies and is now reaching the shores of Asia. May I venture to say, without displaying any more immodesty than the American traveling salesman, that the Japanese civilization has some things to offer you beside silk and yen in exchange for material goods? I do not refer to cherry blossoms, prints, and carving, but to things more difficult to discover and divine. Business men in a hurry to sell us tractors and engines, round-the-world trippers whirling through Japan in ten hours, may overlook them; but if some will come to us without any interest except fine curiosity, and tarry long enough, they may discover imponderable values beyond price.

To give a balanced picture of the background for modern Japan is a difficult task even for us Japanese. Keenly aware of my own lack of qualifications for this task, I made a special effort to prepare myself when I accepted your invitation. I spared no effort in discussing my task with Japanese whose opinions are more worthy than are my own. Before leaving Japan I visited and talked with almost a hundred people, leaders in every sphere of our modern life, with whose aid I hope to give you a realistic picture of the main currents in my country. The choice of materials, of course, lay with me; but in selecting them I have tried to be a fair and impartial judge.

II

I have no intention to attempt to take you through the labyrinth of Japanese history, and make you all anti-Japanese by hurling at your heads such historical names as Saki-no-kampaku-Dajodaijin-Hoshoji-no-nyudo-Fujiwara-no-Yorimichi. This is the full name of one man, you know, and when I was a boy it was considered quite a feat to repeat it all in one breath. On the contrary, I shall start by summarizing as quickly as possible the fundamental elements of the revolution in Japanese society in 1868 which followed the opening of the country by the treaty with the United States in 1858. The men who made that revolution, and their sons, are still among the mighty factors in Japanese foreign and domestic policies. The society which they created remained for half a century "The Old Order of Japan."

In the first place, it must be noted that restoration bears no analogy whatever to the French Revolution which was brought about by the new bourgeois who, assisted by the common people, imposed a constitution upon a monarchy. Our " revolution," if I may say so, was the restoration of the Japanese Emperor to full authority by the arms of powerful feudal lords and a majority of the samurai, or professional warriors of the country.

In the second place, the Japanese restoration instead of destroying feudalism, as did the revolution in France, was itself an expression of revived feudalism. As a great man of letters, the late Fukuchi, said in his history: " It was feudalism that gave the Tokugawa family 260 years of peace, and it was feudalism that destroyed the family in the end." In other words, the shoguns, the Tokugawas, had been unable to crush feudal lords; they ruled by the sword and by the arts of political management. In the end the shogunate was overthrown by a revival of feudalism that wrested power from the Tokugawas, and distributed it among the great lords, under the sovereignty of Emperor Meiji.

In the third place, feudalism was undermined later by the rising power of the nation's merchants who had been growing in prosperity during the Tokugawa régime. Moreover, when feudal tenures were finally abolished, the landlords received government bonds in payment for their rights, and thus, by a strange stroke of history, they became capitalists in one quick transaction. Thus the mercantile bourgeois and the holders of government debentures, instead of being in deadly conflict as were the landlords and bourgeois of England and France, were drawn together in bonds of common economic interest. No profound difference in social psychology separates the clipper of government coupons from the clipper of industrial coupons.

In the fourth place, the abolition of feudal tenures.

when it was effected, did not, as in many European countries, end in an almost complete triumph of a free-holding peasantry. On the contrary, the effect of the abolition was more like that in England where many great landlords continued to hold their estates on a rental or crop-sharing basis. So the feudal clans that had brought about the restoration continued to hold their power, as did the feudal lords of England in the age of the Tudors.

In the fifth place, the main check on the power of the great Japanese lords was the Emperor Meiji, supported by the affection and desires of his people. He saw clearly the danger of that decentralizing and disintegrating feudalism which the Germans call " Zersplitterungswesen." In his policy, he was supported by many wise and far-sighted statesmen who believed that a representative system of government was necessary to offset the power of the great clans. This idea was also popular among those who had studied English and American democracy and were thoroughly imbued with western democratic theories. So among the now famous five articles proclaimed by the young Emperor on March 14, 1869, was one which declared that: " Deliberative assemblies shall be established and all official acts shall be in accord with public opinion." In this article all liberals saw the ringing note of the new spirit. It is my own belief that the leaders at that time had only the vaguest notions regarding the parliamentary systems of the west. It has been said that the article in the Imperial oath never contemplated a parliament by people; at all events, it gave strength to the faith of the rising liberal group that saw in the adoption of democratic political institutions the hope of the future. During this transition, as I shall point out later, many Japanese were in Europe and America zealously studying the art of self-government. Among them was Prince Iwakura, who with his able lieutenants, Okubo, Kido, and Ito, toured the world, and returned to Japan deeply impressed by western progress and firmly convinced that Japan's first need was internal reform.

In the sixth place, the whole course of the Restoration was deeply influenced by foreign affairs and by the education of the new Japanese leaders in the high and mystic arts of foreign diplomacy. It must be remembered that for 216 years Japan had been sealed to foreign nations, that she had devoted her energies to the arts of peace, and that she had left far behind the age of internal wars and foreign conquests. I repeat that this basic fact must not be overlooked by those who would understand Japan today and the position of those Japanese who do not favor so-called "vigorous foreign policies." It was foreign pressure that hastened the overthrow of the shogunate; it was the operations of the foreign powers in China and in Eastern waters that forced the Japanese, whether they liked it or not, to readjust their internal affairs and to seek ways and means to avoid the fate of India and China. So the course of internal progress in Japan, the democratization of Japanese society, could not go on without any thought about foreign policies and national defense.

So from the very beginning, the potential Russells, Gladstones, and Morleys of Japan have had to work under the thundering guns of the Western powers blowing their way to new territories, new empires of trade, new spheres of influence. It is not surprising that they made little headway. One cannot help asking where English democracy would have been if its growth had been conditioned by such circumstances.

I think it will not be necessary for me to apologize therefore for devoting some time to post-Restoration diplomacy. I hope that you will find this part more interesting, especially as the government of the United States and a number of individual Americans played great rôles in formulating that diplomacy.

The remarks I shall make in this connection are based upon the researches of Prof. Katsumaru Nakamura, of the historical department of the Imperial University of Tokyo, who has kindly permitted me to make use of some of his hitherto unpublished materials.

It is important to remember that the foreign policies of Japan since the Restoration have not been those of a small island empire, isolated from the main current of world politics. In reality they have been part and parcel of the world's great political drama. The fall of the Tokugawas was by no means the result of mere internal disturbances, but was made necessary by two outside causes. One cause was the rise of the great Pacific Problem; the other was the Monroe Doctrine of America.

The expansion of the European Powers in the Far East was rapidly advancing in the middle of the nineteenth century. England and France were approaching steadily from the South, while the tentacles of the

Russian octopus were stretching down hungrily from the North. England's position around Hongkong was strengthened enormously by the Nanking Treaty which she signed with China at the conclusion of the Opium War in 1842; while Russia in 1855 signed the Aigun Treaty with the Peking Government and thus acquired the vast territory of the Maritime Province. France occupied Saigon in 1859 and laid the first stone in the foundation of her colonial empire in French Indo-China.

The warships of these three powers had appeared even before this time in the peaceful waters surrounding Japan. Russia invaded Japan's Northern Island in 1805, while British battleships intruded into Nagasaki in 1808. French ships of war reached the Loochoo Islands in 1844. It appeared quite probable that Japan, where peace had reigned for three unbroken centuries, would soon be the scene of a mighty contest between the powers of Europe.

Had either Russia, coming from the North, or England from the South, been given a free hand in Japan, the modern history of the Orient would have been vastly different. The object lessons of Persia and Siam suggest what might have happened. But at this critical moment there arrived on the scene a third party — the American battleships under Commodore Perry, who dropped anchor at Uraga in 1853. The Monroe Doctrine was beginning to spread its beneficent influence over the diplomacy of Asia.

The policy enunciated by President Monroe had closed the American continents to European aggression, and thus had helped turn the eyes of European statesmen towards the Far East for the fulfillment of their ambitions. When, however, Russia and England and France at last reached Japan, they found themselves once more face to face with the same stone wall — the declaration of Monroe with reference to the Pacific.

The Monroe Doctrine had served not only to protect America's eastern shores from Europe but also to expedite her own westward expansion. The Louisiana Purchase, though it preceded the proclamation of the Monroe Doctrine, was prompted by the same spirit, and it was followed by the annexation of Texas, the opening of California and the purchase of Alaska. Still America marched westward.

The tremendous drive of the Slavic race toward the East was perhaps the foremost reason that sent American as well as British battleships to Asiatic waters. The potential power of Russia is perhaps one of the greatest factors that has determined and will continue to determine, the policies of the Pacific Powers.

John Quincy Adams, about a century ago, spoke of the danger of the Pacific's becoming a Russian lake. The concern of the British for the safety of India's northern frontier is well known. The purpose of the Monroe Doctrine would be fulfilled only if the Pacific coast of America were protected fully against the dangers of Slavic expansion. It was the beginning of the contest for supremacy in the Pacific — in other words, the Pacific Problem.

Japan in those days scarcely realized the importance of her own strategic position in this great game. Only America's timely arrival saved the situation for us, a fact for which we shall be eternally grateful. America's presence in the Far East stemmed the tide of European aggression and gave the Japanese reformers a brief time to work at putting their house in order.

Throughout the pre-Restoration period, the danger of foreign intervention had given serious concern to the leaders in the Imperialist cause. England was obviously in sympathy with the Satsuma clan and later with its ally, the Choshu, while France was even more closely associated with the Tokugawas. The young leaders of the reform movement were unafraid of the Shogun's power itself but were genuinely alarmed at the prospect of France's rendering assistance to the Tokugawas.

At the suggestion of certain Britishers, the Satsuma clan decided to send Hohei Iwashita as a representative to the International Exhibition of Paris in 1867. The Shogun's emissaries were headed by his own brother, Shimidzu Mimbu-Tayu. The two hostile groups, meeting in Paris, took advantage of the opportunity to plead their opposing cases before the French Government. France, it was then revealed, realized that the shogunate was no longer in supreme control at home; and the French attitude accordingly became more cautious.

Opinions differ even now regarding the extent of the aid the foreign powers were willing to give the opposing parties, but it may be stated safely that French sympathy was with the Shogun while the British looked favorably upon the Imperialists. A French offer of assistance, made to the Shogun and rejected, is a matter of historical record. Some who sat in the Shogun's councils were in favor of seeking foreign help but the Shogun himself and his best councillors were firm in their opposition to this. They were concerned less with the immediate problem of withstanding the attack of the clans, than with the ultimate effect of foreign intervention on Japan's domestic affairs. The Imperialists also were very cautious in considering the possibility of foreign assistance against the shogunate.

The present generation of Japanese are sincerely grateful for the wisdom with which their ancestors conducted this phase of their relations with foreign countries. The Tokugawas were willing to lose their fight with the clans rather than remain in power with the help of foreign powers. The prudence and discretion of the contending parties, in striking contrast with the revolutionary tactics observed in some neighboring countries, enabled Japan to pass the most crucial period of the Restoration in safety.

The new government of Meiji during the first few years of its existence had no definite foreign policy. The officials were much exercised regarding frontier problems, and Japanese claims for possession of the Loochoo and Bonin Islands were enforced. It proved necessary, on the other hand, to concede Saghalien to Russia in exchange for the Kurile Islands. Japan's relations with Korea were anything but satisfactory. The sending of a punitive expedition to Korea was urged immediately following the Restoration, because Korea had failed to reciprocate the courtesy of the new Government that had sent an official emissary to report the change of regime. The surplus energy of the

Samurai class, however, had quite as much to do with this agitation as the offense taken at Korea's impolite attitude. The episode had no connection whatever with the question that later resulted in the Japanese annexation of Korea and attracted the attention of all the world.

The diplomacy of the restored Imperial Government for half a century revolved about two pivots. In the first place, Japan desired the revision of the treaties she had signed with the foreign powers in 1858, so that she might attain a position of equality among the nations. This I shall discuss later. In the second place, Japan realized the necessity of safeguarding her territorial integrity by the formulation of a definite Asiatic policy.

With the hope of achieving the first of these purposes, Prince Iwakura was sent abroad at the head of a mission in 1871. The mission was unsuccessful, but a curious trick of fate during Iwakura's absence led to the formulation of Japan's continental policy. This policy in definite form came from an American citizen.

General Le Gendre, a Union officer in the American Civil War, after the close of hostilities, was appointed American Consul General at Amoy, China. While assigned to this post, he was obliged on one occasion to visit Formosa, just across the narrow straits, and conduct negotiations with the chiefs of the aborigines there. On his return to Amoy, he sent his Government a dispatch in which he recommended the occupation of the island by the American Navy.

After a period of service at Amoy, General Le Gendre was appointed minister to a South American Republic, and on his way to his new post he passed through Japan. Being introduced by the American Minister to Count Soyeshima, Foreign Minister in the absence of Prince Iwakura, General Le Gendre took occasion to express his views regarding the policies he thought Japan should follow in order to consolidate her position. He impressed upon Soyeshima the menace of Russian aggression from the North, and the danger of British and French designs in the South. The American visitor said, in effect, that Japan would be secure only if she could formulate a continental policy and carry it out before it was too late. He even said that it was the duty as well as the right of Japan.

The policy recommended by General Le Gendre contemplated the expansion of Japanese territory to form a crescent skirting the Asiatic mainland, and embracing both Korea and Formosa, in the North and South respectively. He emphasized the great danger which lurked in the possibility of Russia occupying Korea, and of England or France occupying Formosa. In either of these events, he contended, Japan's security would be seriously threatened. Soyeshima was urged to make the seizure of both Korea and Formosa fundamental in Japan's foreign policy; and as precedents for such a plan, the American official cited the Louisiana Purchase, the annexation of Texas and the acquisition of Alaska by the United States. These steps, he pointed out, had been made necessary by the Monroe Doctrine.

Count Soyeshima was greatly influenced by General Le Gendre's arguments, which also found high favor with Saigo of Satsuma, who had served the Restora-

tion cause with such distinction. Since the Imperial
House had regained its long-lost authority, Saigo had
withdrawn from the public eye and had found himself
frequently in disagreement with the policies of the new
government. Although he was a member of the Cabinet, his opinions frequently were overruled by a majority of his colleagues. When he heard of the new suggestion that had come from an American official, he
was intensely interested and sent his right-hand man,
Kirino, to Soyeshima to obtain a detailed explanation
of Le Gendre's views. The idea fascinated him and
immediately he began to advocate the military occupation of Korea.

The ambitious program was destined, however, to
meet with determined opposition from Prince Iwakura,
who soon returned from his travels with his able lieutenants, Okubo, Kido, and Ito. The great Minister
had been deeply impressed with the progress being
made in western countries and returned home firmly
convinced that Japan's first need was internal reform.
This difference of opinion culminated in the civil war
of 1878, in which Saigo attempted vainly to compel the
adoption of his aggressive views. The Imperial Government emerged from the brief conflict with its position strengthened rather than otherwise.

It was just about this time that another American
assisted in shaping Japan's foreign policy. General
Grant, who was touring the world after the expiration
of his term as President, reached Japan in 1877. The
adoption of a policy of peace was strongly urged in a
long and memorable interview between the former
President and the young Emperor. At the very mo-

ment, a war between China and Japan was pending
over the possession of the Loochoo Islands; but General Grant explained how wars among Asiatic countries
could not fail to advance the plans of European countries. He explained the example and spirit of the
Monroe Doctrine and argued that Japan should
strengthen herself by peaceful means. These calm
views did much to influence the statesmen of Meiji in
formulating their policy. General Grant's advice was
followed and the Japanese house was put in order. It
was only when the Japanese felt fully prepared that
they acted upon Le Gendre's policies, acquiring Formosa in 1895 and Korea in 1910. Thus (in the words
of Professor Nakamura) Japan's Asiatic policy was
thoroughly in accord with the suggestions of two American military men and, to an extent difficult to measure, grew out of their advice. In passing, I may add
that Le Gendre remained a long time in Japan as an
adviser to the Foreign Office. His writings are found
in the official library of the Cabinet.

It is not necessary for me to rehearse before this
audience the story of the Sino-Japanese War or the
Russo-Japanese War or to review the foreign policies of
our own time. Neither do I propose to criticize those
wars or those policies. I hope that I may venture the
suggestion that no spokesman of any of the Great
Powers that have been busy during the past three hundred years, down to the latest moment, conquering and
annexing under the banner of imperialism, has any just
ground for criticizing Japan. A sweeping condemnation
of imperialism and its works, I understand and I respect; but the writer who singles out Japan as the sole

target of his criticism will receive, and I think deserves, no consideration at my hands or the hands of my countrymen. But this is no part of the argument which I desire to lay before you. I have merely sought to show you how vitally foreign affairs have reacted upon our domestic politics. I have tried to explain how the germ of liberal and representative government that sprouted in the early days of the Restoration received little nourishment from the revolution itself. I have endeavored to indicate how it was blasted and withered in the storm that broke when in the name of defence (and certainly not without justification), and following in the wake of the great Western powers, the leaders of the nation turned their energies from domestic reform to " a vigorous foreign policy."

But in the heyday of the vigorous foreign policies of the old order, the unseen hand of fate was busy weaving, away from the gaze of the world, a new brocade for the coming drama of Modern Japan. The germ of liberalism which seemed crushed by the strong hand of conservatives was quietly sprouting. As Spring follows Winter, and Gladstone followed Disraeli, the Japanese liberals were destined to rise once more and valiantly challenge the supremacy of the old order.

LECTURE II

The Challenge of New Forces

THERE was a certain vein of radicalism in the movement that brought about the Restoration of 1868. The young enthusiasts of those days dreamed many a fantastic dream. Their greatest concern was how to avoid the mistake made in 1334 in the restoration of Kemmu when the Hojo Shogunate was overthrown, only to be succeeded by another of the Ashikagas. To prevent this succession, they thought, the only possible means was to strengthen the new government against the feudal lords by inviting the people to share in government. Therefore, the people's restoration was the goal of the new restoration.

During the first few years the policies of the new government tended toward a realization of this program. Gradually, however, the same old reaction began to set in. It came in the shape of foreign policy as was explained in the preceding chapter. The group of statesmen who thought Japan's first duty lay in securing her political integrity rapidly increased their power, and the others who stood for a more radical internal reform had to leave the seat of power one after another. The radical vein of the new government thus steadily faded. Those who left the government naturally went into the ranks of the opposition. These were the men who organized the political parties of Japan.

24

Itagaki organized the Liberal Party, and Okuma the Progressive Party. The former party was more under the influence of French radicalism of the Rousseau school, while the latter drew its inspiration from the liberals of England. The former followers of the defeated Tokugawas also joined these parties. Newspapers were founded to oppose and criticize the activities of the government. Okuma started a college, called Waseda University, while a noted samurai of Tokugawa affiliation started another, Keio University.

The liberals and radicals of those days were intrenched in these new quarters and continued their fight against the government. The first clash of forces came over the question of the proclamation of the constitution. The government took the thunder off their clamor by ordering Ito to draft a new constitution for Japan. It was promulgated in 1889 and the Parliament opened in 1890. The forces of democracy fought the government by this new political weapon, but the internal and international situation was against them. The conservatives who ruled the country were men of no small talents. They were constructive and moderately progressive. They gave the people prosperity at home and security abroad. People preferred the constructive policies of these conservatives to the high-sounding ideals of the radicals. There was another fundamental reason for the failure of the liberals of those days to arouse the enthusiasm of the common people; namely, that both the ministerialists and the opposition belonged to the same social class. It was mainly a case of people who had belonged to the samurai class in the feudal days carrying on a factional fight for power in the new day. There was no particular reason why the opposition should be considered as representing the interest of the common people. The latter preferred, on the contrary, the sane progress under the old order to the wild agitation of the radicals.

There was another strong weapon that the conservatives used to bolster up their position. That was the educational system of new Japan. The progress of modern Japan is due to the success of its educational system more than to anything else — particularly to its public education. In forty years it diminished the percentage of illiteracy to less than five per cent of the whole population; the school attendance of the children of school age in 1923 was 99.03 per cent. A highly competitive system of examinations was practiced in the schools. The best brains were competing to get into the government school, as those who stood well in examinations were given recognition by the general public. At the apex of the whole system were the imperial universities. The students all vied with one another to reach the top; and once in the university, they competed with an intense passion to stand well in its examinations. Those who got honors in the examinations were given state recognition and their future careers were assured. Into the mind of the student was thus instilled a strong nationalism; and the graduates of these government universities went mostly into government service where, owing to a very strict civil service system, everybody had a chance to get recognition of his talent. Contrary to the notion accepted abroad, Japan is a country where a poor man's son has a fair chance of promotion — due to this strict com-

petitive system. No political pull or family connection works there. Through the system the conservative rulers of the land skillfully skimmed the cream
of the nation and invited into the government the
ablest talents who would otherwise have joined the
opposition. This was the secret of the endurance of
the old order and the weakness of the liberal opposition.

The World War changed the whole situation. The
prosperity that came to Japanese business and industry during the war created a strong and prosperous
middle class, which gradually began to agitate for a
change in politics. From 1916 to 1918 the tide of
liberalism began to rise. Leaders of liberal views became more and more popular. It was also the time
when the voices of men like Wilson were ringing all
over the world. The political current of Japan began
to swell high. In the field of actual politics people de-
manded more liberal policies. The preponderance of
the executive branch of the government was challenged
and the power of the legislative branch began to increase. The upshot of the whole thing was the demand
for the extension of the suffrage as a domestic reform
and for the change of Japan's continental policy, especially in relation to China. In March, 1925, the universal manhood suffrage law passed both houses of the
parliament and ten million new voters were added to
the old three million. In 1922, Japan decided to fall
in line with America and return the remaining part of
the Boxer indemnity, accruing to her, to China. This
amounts to seventy-three million yen, or thirty-six and
one-half million dollars gold. In harmony with a program, called " Cultural Work in China," the whole

amount will be used to help advance the civilization of China. The first appropriation of 5,350,000 yen was granted by the July session of the Parliament of 1924. This will be spent in six years for the creation of two institutes of research in Peking and Shanghai. The one in Peking will be devoted to research in the fields of philosophy, literature, and social science; the one in Shanghai to research in the field of natural sciences. These institutes are not to be confined to Chinese and Japanese scholars, but their doors will be wide open to all properly qualified foreigners; their findings are to be published in Western languages. Japan has also declared on every occasion her intention to keep aloof from any policy of intervention in Chinese domestic affairs.

Thus the economic changes that began to take place in Japan in recent years have already changed her internal and international policies. The vigorous foreign policy adopted at the early stage of the new regime is fast being modified. The rising tide of liberalism is making a steady advance on the citadels of conservatism and the strong nationalistic policy is being toned down. The reason why liberalism failed in the early days was because it lacked the sympathy of the common people. This time it sprang from the consciousness of the people and was not the slogan of a few politicians. How this liberal spirit was being formulated in the field of thought will be discussed in the next chapter.

When the tide of liberalism was rising in Japan, another great change was following close at its heels. It was the sudden rise of the power of labor. The

business boom that came to Japan after 1915, the second year of the Great War, sent wages soaring to the
sky, or at least so it seemed to the long-underpaid
Japanese labor. With the increase of wages came the
consciousness of power. A labor movement began to
figure highly in Japanese public life. Since the rise of
the power of labor was sudden, it lacked leaders at
first from its own ranks. Naturally, students of labor
problems, men of socialistic affiliations, assumed direction of the labor movement. Now socialism had an unfortunate history in Japan. In 1910 socialists were in-
volved in a plot against the Imperial Family and were
strictly prohibited from propaganda. They lived in
obscurity. In the heyday of the labor movement they
suddenly came out of their life of hibernation into open
daylight. The Russian Revolution of 1917 stimulated
the interest of young Japan and adherents of socialism
swelled in numbers. The industrial workers gradually
came under its spell. From 1917 on, Japan began to
witness a great number of sensational strikes — mark-
ing such a change from the solid, compact nation bent
on the prosecution of a vigorous continental policy.
From 1919 to 1922 radical syndicalists were the leaders of the organized labor of Japan. In 1922, in September, the national conference of labor unions was
won over by the leaders of communistic affiliations; in
October, 1923, leadership passed to reform socialists
somewhat like those of the British labor party. In the
days of the syndicalistic and communistic ascendency,
Japanese labor ruled political activities out of their
program. Their only weapon was direct action. Now
with the realization of the universal manhood suffrage

they are preparing to fight their cause with the new political weapon of parliamentary representation.

A more important phase, in a way, of the Japanese labor situation is the agrarian movement. According to the census of 1920, 67 per cent of the population of Japan lived in rural districts; two thirds of the population was engaged in agriculture. When the boom of industry sent the prices of manufactured goods skyward those of farm produce were slow to follow. That made the position of the farmers rather difficult. Good days came a little later, it is true, but they did not last long. Agricultural conditions became more serious. Japan is a hilly country, and the total arable land amounts to only 15 per cent of the national area. This means that Japan has to support 969 persons by one square kilometre of cultivated land, whereas Belgium has thus to support only 394, Italy 305, Netherlands 273, and England 226. The land in Japan is divided among small landowners. When the business slack came after the war and the cost of living did not go down accordingly, the condition of the Japanese peasant became impossible to bear. Farming ceased to be a paying undertaking. Two-thirds of the Japanese farmers are tenants who till the leased land of others; therefore the Japanese agrarian problem is a tenant problem. Violent methods were used by these desperate tenants at first, but gradually they began to use the more effectual method of an organized movement. How these tenants are going to move ultimately in their political and economic agitation cannot be foreseen, but it is quite within the limit of reasonable speculation to predict that they will not go the

way of industrial workers. In the first place, because
of the nature of their work they are more conservative;
and secondly, they have been better trained politically.
The strongholds of the Japanese political parties were
always in the rural districts and, in consequence, the
farmers are more used to attaining their ends by political means than are industrial workers. The agrarian
movement will be a more important factor in deciding
the political future of Japan, at least in the coming
twenty or thirty years. In the contest of the liberals
and socialists for leadership over the newly-emanci-
pated masses of people, rural districts will hold the
balance of power and decide the outcome.

If the economic pressure continues to tighten and
drives the rural districts of Japan to vote more radical
tickets, the political situation will gradually resemble
that of Great Britain; namely, the clean-cut conflict
between capital and labor. If, on the other hand, the
government succeeds in finding an economic solution
for the people at large and particularly for the agrarian
labor, the latter will continue to support the constructive policies of the liberals. The Japanese have a
curious aversion to extremity. Moderation is the
virtue we cherish, sometimes to an immoderate degree.
Frankly admitting the seriousness of the economic conditions in town and country, I still believe that a way
will be found to bridge over the difficult period of
transition.

In sixty years, Japan has spent the vigor and force
of the spirit of the Restoration of 1868. We have
reached a point where the internal and international
policies are all to be overhauled. The population has

increased from thirty to sixty millions in these sixty years, and the situation of the whole world has changed. Japan now stands at the crossroads. Economically she has no choice. Industrialization is her only way forward. Her only concern is how she can avoid some of the mistakes committed by other nations. The strength of the Japanese nation lies in her agrarian population. To my mind, a decentralization of industries, by which the interdependence of industries and agriculture can be worked out, is one of the possible solutions of her social plight.

There is another phase to the future changes of the Japanese policies; that is the question whether Japan will be driven to a purely Oriental policy and theatre of operations, or whether she will be brought forward to a closer coöperation with the whole world. The answer will depend, not on the future development in Asiatic politics, but more on the attitude of the Western nations toward the Eastern races.

LECTURE III

INTELLECTUAL CURRENTS IN JAPAN

I

BROADLY speaking, there are five schools of ethical and religious conviction that are living forces in Japanese life: Shintoism, Confucianism, Buddhism, Bushido, and, quite recently, Christian teachings. How systems acted and reacted on one another, and what will be their future course, is a most interesting subject for anyone eager to understand the social and political development of the East. It will be particularly interesting to Americans who have sent most of the missionaries to Japan, to understand what rôle Christianity is going to play in that country and eventually in the whole East.

In studying the history of the development of ethical and religious systems in Japan, the following characteristics will attract the attention of a careful student. It is these national traits which have functioned in the past and will continue to function in the future, that will shape the intellectual currents in the first instance and the political and social policies of the country in the end.

In the first place, the Japanese people are exceedingly quick to accept foreign ideas. This receptive power, which sharply marks the Japanese from the Chinese, has been the source of much sarcasm directed against Japanese by a number of foreign observers. They have called it "imitation" and in some cases, an "apish mimicry." Without going into the discussion of whether there is any categorical difference between imitation and originality, I shall content myself with saying that the real test in the case should be whether the receiver ends by contributing something to the great social heritage of mankind, or not. This adaptability of the Japanese to new ideas has helped them to graft to their own stock, branches of different schools of philosophy and religion that later sent forth flowers of different fragrances and hues from the original.

The receptive power of the Japanese nation would have been of rather little avail in its spiritual development, had it not been accompanied by another trait, that is, the power of digestion. This is where casual observers have utterly failed to understand Japan. By looking at the temples and pagodas in Japan they have hastily rushed to the conclusion that Japanese Buddhism was the same as in China. Then again by noticing the tall office buildings and noisy automobiles in Tokyo, they have written down in their charming impressions of the East that Japan had been thoroughly occidentalized. They did not take the trouble to find out that in each of these temples there sat a Japanese priest, and that under each of the silk hats there was concealed a Japanese head!

The discrimination and digestion that accompany the adoption of new ideas in Japan are to be explained by the fact that every new thought encounters great resistance at the time of its introduction. This capacity for quick reception and quick opposition, although

at first seemingly paradoxical, has helped the progress
of the Japanese people. Confucianism in the third century, and Buddhism in the sixth century, underwent
the same process at the time of their introduction.
This is a very remarkable phenomenon and needs
some explanation, as it throws a light on Japanese
psychology and also helps us to divine the future
course of Christianity in Japan.

When Buddhism was first introduced into Japan
from Korea in 552 A.D., it brought about a commotion
in the minds of the ruling class. From the Emperor
down to the lowliest retainer, the Japanese were affected by the novel idea. But gradually there appeared
among the great ministers in the court a strong resistance which was not put to an end until after some
bloodshed. However, the real resistance was not the
mere outside opposition of the politicians, but was
rather in the disturbed minds of the thinkers of those
days. They could not reconcile the ideas of Buddhism
with the ruling thought of Japan inherited from their
ancestors. The idea of putting Buddha above all other
gods was in contradiction to the idea of Shintoism,
which recognized the Sun Goddess as the supreme
Guardian Deity of Japan. This was not solved until the
great priest Gyoki in the eighth century formulated a
new interpretation of Buddhism by saying that Buddha
and the Sun Goddess were not different personalities.
When the Creator appeared in India, she took the form
of Buddha and there was no innate difference in spirit
nor teaching. Gyoki thus removed the troublesome
obstacle, and paved the way for the reconciliation
of Buddhism and Shintoism, which secured for Bud-

dhism unmolested progress in the country. The same
thing can be said of Confucianism, Taoism, and the
teachings of other foreign thinkers. It is only half
a century since Christianity was introduced after a
long period of suppression. That faith is now passing
through the same stage in Japan through which other
teachings have passed; and I very much doubt whether
Christianity as developed in America and Europe will
be accepted as such by large numbers of the Japanese.
The same tenacious resistance is being seen; and Christianity, in my opinion, will not make much headway
in Japan unless its teachers are reconciled to the fact
that the Japanese will not accept a foreign thought
without impressing upon it their own stamp.

The third trait, which is more or less connected
with the above, is the Japanese love of harmony. I am
rather inclined to think that the main difference between the East and the West springs from their different attitudes toward harmony. Individual liberty
has been accentuated in the West and it is undoubtedly
the foundation of Western progress, while in the East,
at least in Japan, the foundation of moral ideas has
been harmony. It is not mere collectivism — it is
more the love of harmony. Everything in the Universe must find itself in perfect harmony with the
whole. A thing is always valued at the position it
holds in the whole plan of the Universe. This love of
harmony always drove the Japanese to an attempt to
connect each new thought with the ideas already accepted. Confucianism had to fit in with the indigenous
thought of Shintoism; and Buddhism again had to be
reconciled with the two systems of thought that existed

there. This tendency to seek harmony can be found in all the great thinkers of Japan. They have not been like Protestants and Catholics and Christians and Mohammedans. Instead of fighting for supremacy and trying to stamp out the opposition, Japanese philosophers and ethical teachers have sought a way to forge all different systems of thought into one harmonious whole. That tendency is clearly seen in Japan at present in the efforts to bring together the leaders of three different religions. I dare say that you recently read in the newspapers the story of Japanese Shinto, Buddhist, and Christian leaders meeting for coöperation. It doubtless looks very queer to you, but it is the national trait of Japan. We do things in our own way.

This quest for harmony among thinkers is the spirit of tolerance, and it is the reason why we are not good haters. It is a weakness as well as a strength. It tends to soften down bold and confident personalities and it blurs the sense of distinction. But at the same time, it enables us to avoid much of the unnecessary waste that comes from fighting over things which are not very important.

We have harmonized all exotic thought with our indigenous idea of Shintoism. Now it remains to be seen how the three new ideas that are fermenting in the Western world are going to be Japanized and incorporated into Japanese thought; I mean, Christianity, Democracy, and Socialism.

The fourth outstanding characteristic of the Japanese is the love of action, or the predominance of the theory of action in contradiction to the theory of existence or the pure metaphysical reflection.   All the Japanese ethical systems of thought have the stamp of conduct.   A philosophy for a Japanese is not a pure system of metaphysical thought, but is a thing that is to be translated into daily conduct.   Knowledge is not real knowledge until you act on it.   The philosophy of the great teacher, Zinsai Ito (1627–1705), is the most typical illustration of the Japanese mode of thinking.   He glorified action and expounded the theory that the Universe exists by and for action.   The goal of his action was benevolence and justice.   Action exists for action itself and not for any recognition to be won from others. He explained the order of Heaven, declaring that when a man believes in the order of Heaven and never loses his peace of mind on account of outward honors or criticisms, he can be said to have reached the state of a sage.   To *do* one's utmost and leave the result to the order of Heaven is a precept that has constituted a fundamental ethical idea of the Japanese.   The philosopher Ito in his lifetime had three thousand disciples; and one of these three thousand was the famous Oishi, the head of the forty-seven ronins.

This Japanese love of action is clearly seen in their leaning toward Wan-Yang-Ming's philosophy, which places action above all things; and also in their taking Christianity very seriously.   In Japan Christianity is construed in a very strict sense, and when a man does not drink or smoke people will ask him whether he is not a Christian.   Here is the sign of our belief in the theory of conduct.   Everything you believe you are expected to translate into your daily conduct.

Another trait of the Japanese is his optimism.   Even

Buddhism with all its quiet pessimism could not change this national trait. The philosophy of the Japanese nation is optimism. The mild climate, the fortunate geographic situation that has spared them the misery of a foreign yoke, and the spirit of tolerance, which sprang up among them, all tended to make them cheerful and optimistic. The joy of life is vibrant in their blood and their ethical opinions run along that line. This was given the best expression by the philosopher and the first popular educator of Japan, Yokiken Kaibara, who lived from 1630 to 1714.

The Japanese by nature are not good philosophers. They are more artistic than scientific, and are not given to abstract meditation. Their philosophies of life have not culminated in great and complicated systems of thought. They tended to become simple and informal. The great teacher of Shintoism, Norinaga Motoori (born 1730, died 1801), said that in Japan there was no necessity for any system of morals, as every Japanese acted aright if only he consulted his own heart. It was not so much any philosophy or system of morals that counted among the Japanese, as the fact that they could lead contented and peaceful lives as individuals and as a nation for many centuries; and they have shown a spirit of strong resistance whenever their peace of mind and peace of community life have been disturbed by foreign opinions alien to their mode of life. New ideas could find a permanent place only after they were adjusted to Japanese life and thus served to strengthen and perpetuate the individual and community life of the country.

In this connection I should like to give a brief sketch

of the ethical ideas of Motoori, as he is considered by many as one of the great teachers whose thought inspired the Restoration of Meiji in 1868. His views are also important in giving a clue to the original Japanese view of life, which served as the ethical foundation of the country.

He attributed all the phenomena of the world to the will of God, and said that the duty of man consisted in carrying out the divine will. As for guidance in ascertaining that divine will, he pointed to the sincere heart of man given to him by God.

Motoori then laid down four cardinal rules of conduct:

1. To live a peaceful life by contentedly carrying out one's daily duties.

2. Always to keep purity of heart.

3. To revere one's ancestors.

4. To make the Emperor's will one's own will and reverently to obey him.

These precepts are important in the sense that again and again they come back with the revival of the national spirit. These views are also seen constituting the basis for the nationalism of Meiji whch I will explain later in this lecture.

II

When we consider the moral code of the Japanese nation, the word Bushido comes into the minds of many. We owe the enunciation of this idea for the outside world to the great work by Professor Nitobe, whose humble disciple I am. There is, therefore, no need on my part to dwell on that any more. The thing to which

I want to call your attention is the fact that whereas Bushido furnished a great code of morals for the Bushi or warriors who were the aristocracy of those days, there were other teachings which furnished codes of morals for the masses — for Democracy.

In my first lecture I referred to the fact that the downfall of the Tokugawa shogunate was being prepared by the changing fabric of society. In the end of the shogunate new social forces were rising and challenging the supremacy of the samurai or warriors. The merchant class, which during three centuries of unbroken peace had been gradually accumulating wealth, finally menaced the economic system of feudalism which rested on landed aristocracy, composed of the Bushi or warriors. Along with material wealth, the merchant class acquired cultural attainments. And this culture of the lower class of people was furnished by a number of great teachers who turned their attention from teaching warriors to educating the new emancipated mass of people. The first popular educator, Yokiken Kaibara (1630–1714), expounded the difficult Confucian teachings with the plainest of words and wrote over a hundred books that went into the hands of the poor. Even greater than this was the influence of the famous Baigan Ishida (born 1685, died 1744). He started his career as a clerk in a shop in Kyoto, and wound up his life as a great teacher for the newly rising Democracy. His teachings were based on the three great systems of Shintoism, Buddhism, and Confucianism. Those who belonged to this school of teaching took particular pains to make it easy to understand. In sharp contrast to the writing of the teachers of the aristocracy, their style was easy to follow and their books spread all over the country. Even now the books by these teachers are most interesting reading, enlivened as they are by allegories and fables, and splashed with genial humour.

Then again there was another great teacher whose power was strongest among peasants. He was called a peasant-sage and his teachings are a living force even now, not only among peasants but also among intellectuals. The name of the teacher was Sontoku Ninomiya, and he lived from 1787 to 1856. His teachings were very practical and concrete, and wherever his teachings are well observed the peasant class is very well-to-do and public-spirited. The present minister of education belongs to this school of thought.

The way was well paved by these teachers for the arrival of a new epoch; and it was no wonder that the Japanese people — not only the aristocratic samurai but the democratic masses as well — were ready for the new adventure in statecraft when the country was opened to the world in 1868.

III

When the gate of the great dam was opened after the three long centuries, the flood of Western learning rushed into the Island Empire with stupendous velocity and volume. It looked as though the intellectual life of the whole country was to be submerged by occidental philosophies. Everybody turned to the new ideas; and for the moment Buddhism, Shintoism, and Confucianism were all thrown to the winds.

Gradually, however, the same old resistance to new

ideas began to assert itself. First narrow-minded chauvinism and finally sane, well-balanced criticism began
to loom up over the inundation of Western thought.
This reaction culminated in the latter part of the Meiji
era in the consolidation of a new system of thought,
that is, the nationalism. The basic principles of Shintoism — loyalty to the Emperor, the idea of national
unity and exalted views of the founding of the country
— were formulated into a new theory of the state with
the assistance of the newly imported ideas of nationalism in the Western sense, particularly the German
school of thought along the Hegelian philosophy, ideal-
izing the state. It was systematically taught in schools,
and through books, speeches, and newspapers. All
Japanese who were educated in those days bear its mark
in a very strong degree. Other ideas that did not attune
to this idea of nationalism were looked upon with sus-
picion, if not antagonism. It was with this strong nationalistic spirit that we went into wars with China and
Russia, and finally into the Great War of 1914–1918.

But underneath the apparent undisputed supremacy
of Nationalism, there were other systems of thought
being prepared quietly but steadily. These emphasized, for instance, the idea of individuality advanced
by Christian teachings, and the non-resistance theory
of the Tolstoyan school. The remarkable popularity
of Russian literature, particularly the writings of Tolstoy, had a great deal of influence with the young men
of Japan; and unconsciously the way was being paved
for changing the psychology of the nation. It needed
only changes in the world of affairs to bring these new
forces into action.

The changes came with the World War. The speeches of the statesmen of the allied and associated powers were real propaganda for liberalism and democracy. Liberals at home became bolder and more active. Utterances of men like Professor Nitobe and Professor Yoshino were stamped by the government with the brand of dangerous thoughts; but they kept on increasing their adherents. The years from 1916 to 1918 were marked by a nationwide discussion of liberalism and democracy, although Japan was then under the premiership of the conservative statesman, Terauchi. Those who belonged to the old nationalist school found it more and more difficult to arouse enthusiasm among the people. Many books bearing the title of "Democracy" appeared, and newspapers and magazines were full of articles on the subject. This tendency was capitalized by the shrewd Hara who, organizing his cabinet in the fall of 1918, posed as the first Commoner Premier at the head of a real party government. It caught the imagination of the people, and the liberal opinion of Japan was solidly behind him. During the first half of his administration he really served the cause of Liberalism by removing the restrictions on press, publication, and speech. His internal and international policies were also liberal. But it was not the changes in the field of politics that accelerated the onward march of liberalism in Japan. It was the economic changes, as I stated in my second lecture, that created an independent and prosperous middle class. But there was another element. That was the rapid growth of journalism in those days. Newspapers and magazines increased their circulations by leaps and bounds. This made them financially stronger, and in turn encouraged the growth of a new class of people, i.e., the independent writers.

Before the days of the economic prosperity of 1916–1919, independent writers in Japan were in a most unenviable position. Even a popular novelist found it difficult to keep his body and soul together. Many, in fact, died in misery. The situation was so piquantly epitomized by the famous Ryoku-u, or the Green Rain, in his undying words, " Why, the pen of a writer is one in number, while his chopsticks are two. No wonder that he is so hopelessly outnumbered! " The essayists were in a far worse position than the novelists. They could not make a living without some kind of salary.

Now in the heyday of Japanese journalism came days of prosperity and power for writers and novelists. Their books sold by the thousand and there were constant and ever-increasing demands for articles. The prices of these articles went up by leaps and bounds. Writers for the first time found out that they could fight two chopsticks with one pen. Now independent writers are always very dangerous opponents of conservative rulers. When their bread and butter is secure beyond the reach of the police and rich employers, then they sharpen their pens against the wrongs of the existing society. This universal tendency began to work among the Japanese writers. They began to get bolder and more outspoken. The intellectual currents of Japan began to flow swiftly and in swelling volume. Nationalism was challenged on its supreme throne of immunity. Liberalism and Democracy made

a steady advance on the citadel of the conservative
doctrine of the state and the constitution; and accepted
historical traditions were put to the severe test of
searching, scientific criticism. The hundred-page article of Professor Yoshino on the meaning of Democracy, which appeared in the New Year's number of the
Central Review, a popular magazine, started a great
discussion among the thinkers of the country. A new
theory of the state emerged from the controversy, and
promised to supersede the old one.

At this juncture, the conservatives woke up one fine
morning and found still more dangerous foes walking
into the scene of battle. They were socialism, syndicalism and anarchism. The growing force of labor
on one side and the example of the social revolution
in Russia on the other, strengthened the hands of the
radical thinkers in Japan; and they came out of their
long hibernation into the open daylight. They laughed
at the lukewarm attitude of the liberals and preached
the doctrine of fire. Extreme ideas are always fascinating to young men and many of the advocates of
liberalism were gradually converted to the cause of
socialism. From 1919 to 1922 the socialistic writers
had the ears of the nation, and newspapers and magazines were full of articles on socialism, on Karl Marx,
on Lenin, and so forth. It led the outside observers to
wonder whether a social revolution were coming in
Japan. The thing they overlooked was the strong
resistance that was bound to come later against all
these new and radical ideas; and the reaction came with
the earthquake of 1923.

The national calamity sobered the minds of Japanese and they began to look at things from a new angle. They realized that in the days of uncertainty and suffering after the earthquake, the thing that helped them most was not high-sounding ideas but hard-headed practical work. They realized also that they were greatly reduced in wealth and power, and that they could not afford to play with extreme theories any more. Then it dawned upon them that the one thing that would help them was not the half-digested foreign ideas, but the indigenous ethics of the country, which had served them through dark and trying days.

The intellectual currents made another turn. The pendulum of opinion was swinging back to a more traditional line of thought. It sometimes looked as though Japanese thinkers were returning to the same old reactionary nationalism. Particularly during the first few weeks following the disaster, when there were no newspapers and martial law reigned in the devastated area, the intellectual atmosphere was gloomy with the reactionary spirit.

But with the return of the newspapers, brighter days came back. In fact, the press was restored with increased circulations and increased vigor. The problem of reconstruction brought about a new line-up of people in two opposing camps. The dismal failure of the old type of politician disappointed the people. Radicals began to see the need of working with the moderate liberals, and the intellectual currents of the country began to take on a practical and constructive tone.

The Immigration Act of the United States broke upon us at this very moment. It swept the whole coun-

try like a hurricane. All the papers were unanimous in
protesting against it. At first it seemed as though it
were going to affect only the political sphere. It gradually began to go deeper. It made a tremendous impression on the thinking part of the nation. The disappointment with the West drove them to turn to
their old schools of thought for enlightenment. Ori-
entalism received a new stimulus; and I think I am
not mistaken in saying that there will rise, with the new
scientific method of the West, a greater and deeper desire for the study of Oriental culture. What kind of new
thought will emerge, nobody is yet in a position to
predict.

IV

The trend of opinion is formulated in many ways.
But in our modern age the first place of importance
must be given to newspapers. Now Japanese newspapers are in a very strong position. Very few people
in foreign countries know that Japanese papers are
next to only American and English papers in their circulations. The Osaka *Mainichi* has a daily circulation
of one million and a quarter; and combined with the
sister paper, the Tokyo *Nichi Nichi* under the same
management enjoys the circulation of two millions.
The Tokyo *Asahi* and the Osaka *Asahi* under the same
ownership come pretty near the above figure. There
are a number of other papers that have about half a million readers. As a political power, a business proposi-
tion, or an intellectual organ, the newspaper holds a
position not to be lightly considered. I think the day
will come before long, when the world will take more
notice of the significance of the Japanese press.

The number of Japanese papers exceeded eleven hundred in 1920; and I think that by a conservative estimate, their total circulation must be between six and seven millions. So it can safely be said that of the eleven million families in Japan, half of them take a paper every day. The percentage of illiteracy is very small in Japan, possibly under 5% of all the population. You will be surprised at the extent to which the papers are read by the laboring class. You will notice practically every rickshaw man reading a paper while waiting for a customer. It is by the papers that Japan's democracy is being educated and supported.

Because of their tremendous circulation, Japanese newspapers are great business enterprises. The leading papers in both Tokyo and Osaka have magnificent buildings five to eight stories high, and their annual outlay reaches several millions. The fact that the Tokyo *Asahi* spends as much a year for foreign cables as the London *Times,* will give you an idea of its nature and standing. A few years ago a group of people started a newspaper in Osaka with two million yen of capital and lost all their money within a year and retired. Such are the financial risks of great journalism. You would also be surprised to learn how much advertising Japanese papers secure from American business firms, but I am not at liberty to give you the names and the amount that is spent.

Some outstanding features of the Japanese press will not be altogether uninteresting:

In the first place, the major portion of the proceeds of the Japanese newspapers is derived from the sale of papers and not from the advertisements, which in

America constitute 90% of all the income of news-papers. The *Hochi* of Tokyo received 43% of its income from advertisements in 1922 and the rest from the sale of papers. This gives a peculiar feature to the papers themselves. It gives them an independence from big business men who place advertisements with them. This accounts for the peculiar spirit of independence that runs through their columns. They write freely about capital, labor, and government, foreign governments included. Japanese who spend some time in foreign countries deplore the freedom of the Japanese press, particularly in regard to the foreign countries.

Japanese papers, in the second place, differ in their size from American and English papers. They are mostly eight pages; sometimes they run to fourteen pages. They resemble in that respect French papers. They are very easily read. But with such a meagre amount of space, a little less than half is given to the advertisements.

In the substance of the articles, they are again different from your papers. They give less attention to news and quite a great deal to what we call "leisure articles"; for instance, literature, poetry, long series of essays by college professors, explanations of "Go" (Japanese chequers), and Japanese chess. And every paper carries from two to three serial novels, running from one to twelve months. It is partly due to the Japanese love of literature, but there is also a pathetic side to it. Owing to the pressing daily needs, most of the Japanese people cannot afford to spend evenings in delightful movies or automobile rides, and the only meagre recreation they can contrive to get is by reading stories and poems in the dailies after their work is done.

Another aspect of the Japanese press which foreigners fail to notice is the fact that a paper with political affiliations never succeeds in Japan. *Chuo,* the official organ of the Seiyukai, could never succeed in gaining a large circulation even during twenty years of the party's ascendency. The circulation of the popular paper *Mancho* suddenly dropped off when it decided to support the Okuma ministry in 1914. Therefore, the Japanese papers make it their policy to be cautiously independent of political parties and the government. They sell better when they are in the opposition.

The success of the Japanese papers is all the more remarkable when we consider the disadvantages under which they have struggled. Such handicaps are numerous.

The first handicap is the limitations created by press law. It gives the police authorities the power to stop the sale of particular copies, and also gives the Home Office the right to suppress the publication itself. Although these powers are not used often, they stand as a constant menace to the press.

In the second place, Japanese papers have to employ three times as many reporters as the American papers. The reasons are threefold: The imperfect state of communication and correspondence, the reluctance of the general public to give news, and lastly, the unsatisfactory organization of the news agency business.

Japanese newspapers are greatly burdened by the necessity of delivering their papers to the houses of nearly all their subscribers. About fifteen million yen is spent by the papers annually for the piecemeal delivery of the papers.

Then there is the great handicap of the using of Chinese characters. We use some ten thousand of these for literary and scholarly work. Our written language consists of complex Chinese characters, and simple Japanese syllabaries of which there are only forty-seven. And, until quite recent times, the newspapers had to keep at least nine thousand of these Chinese characters. They have gradually cut down the number, however, and are now using some two thousand; but even then the types used by the *Hochi* for twelve pages of paper are seven million while those for English and American papers with twenty pages are only between 750,000 and 1,000,000. Because of this intricate business of using Chinese characters along with the Japanese syllabaries the Japanese papers cannot use high-speed machines. And yet a paper like *Hochi* prints eleven editions a day. There is now a movement in Japan to restrict the number of Chinese characters and write mostly with the simple Japanese syllabaries. It is proposed to cut them down to six hundred. Then the children of Japan will be saved all the agony of memorizing five or six thousand characters, and incidentally the newspapers will cut down their expenses.

In conclusion, I may say that the Japanese newspapers are increasing in power, and they will be the mainstay of the Japanese liberalism. As they have taken particular pains to be independent of the Government and have espoused the cause of the readers, which means the common people, they may be a great instrument for bridging over the crucial time of transition through which we are now passing.

V

Now, en passant, I must touch briefly on the Japanese magazines, which have some peculiarities of their own. We have over four thousand of them excluding those published for members only. Some popular magazines, and particularly those for ladies, have circulations somewhere near three hundred thousand. We have not a *Saturday Evening Post* yet, but we have many magazines like the *Review of Reviews* and *World's Work*.

One aspect that is rather unique in Japan is the popularity of serious and radical magazines. In this group fall two magazines which are by far the best in Japan, i.e., the *Reconstruction* and the *Central Review*, each of which has a circulation somewhere between sixty and seventy thousand. If you study the contents of *Reconstruction,* you will be surprised at the great extent of its circulation. Take the August number for instance. An article of twenty-five pages entitled " From the Society of Free Acquisition to the Society of Capitalistic Exploitation " by a famous economist; then thirteen pages on the bi-cameral system in legislatures; an article on the artistic philosophy of Deltai; twenty pages on the " Reasons for the Decay of Civilization " and so on. These are all scholarly treatises. *Reconstruction* is a more radical magazine than the *New Republic* or the *Nation.* It prints in every number at least one article by an eminent Western writer, like Bertrand Russell, Kautzky, or H. G. Wells. Yet it enjoys a circulation of over sixty or seventy thousand. It also prints two to six short stories of very high artistic value.

All the Japanese magazines of first-rate standing print long essays by scholars. Their subscribers are particularly fond of reading philosophical studies of from fifty to one hundred pages.

Another feature of the high-class magazines is the publication of novels and short stories of undoubted merit.

The success of the magazines augments in no small degree the increasing influence of independent writers. They are, in fact, mostly radical writers, socialistic writers being rather more popular because they can make bolder assertions than the liberals.

Still I must conclude by saying that Japan is like England and France, and that the dailies are more powerful and prosperous than the magazines.

Now I want to say a few words about publications other than periodicals. Books are not so successful in Japan as newspapers or magazines. The greatest sale on record is perhaps that of " Human Bullet," an autobiography of a young lieutenant at the siege of Port Arthur during the Russo-Japanese War. It sold half a million copies in twenty years. In recent years " Beyond the Death Line," a story of an earnest social worker, sold over two hundred thousand in a few years, and the drama entitled " The Priest and the Disciples " had the same success. But as a rule books do not go beyond a few thousand.

VI

Whither goes Japan then with all these new intellectual equipments? People talk about Japan in transition; but all nations are passing through a period of transition all the time. There is no particular transition for Japan at this particular moment. However, if we accept that terminology for convenience's sake we can, roughly speaking, say that Japan is going through the period of foreign influence into a new one of formulating and consolidating her own thought. Intellectual currents of Japan are taking a new turn in that respect, and there are some landmarks to indicate the trend.

1. The first landmark is the passing of enthusiasm for works translated from foreign languages. Japan has long been under the influence of translations, and the bookshops were long full of the works of American and European authors. But now the publishers are not very keen to print many translated works. The Japanese are turning to their own masters. The sowing has been done and the people are now preparing for the harvesting.

2. The passing of the age of translations meant the coming of the new study of Japan herself. The West taught Japan the scientific method of research, which she is going to apply to her own culture and the institutions bequeathed by her ancestors. New researches in Japanese history with special reference to politics, social changes, economics, literature, ethical thought, and all kinds of institutions, are recasting our fundamental ideas. We now look at our past with new eyes and find that there are some things in the course of our

natural development that we had not realized before. It also opens a new road for original thinking.

3. Then changes in the style of language facilitate the progress of the new orientation. We are getting away from our bondage to the Chinese classics. Our style is growing less and less formal; greater liberty is given to the free play of one's thought and imagination.

It is particularly striking in the case of children and young students. Their brains are taxed less with tortuous cramming in Chinese and Japanese classics as well as foreign languages, whereas until a decade ago study meant memorizing thousands of Chinese characters and idioms. The emancipation from stereotyped characters has meant the liberation of spirit. The way the young children of Japan now write is surprising. There is a new note of free thinking untrammeled by Chinese idioms. In my student days, which are not very far away, our supreme task was to commit to memory thousands and thousands of Chinese idiomatic expressions used in ancient literature and poems, because otherwise we could not write with distinction. The free spirit that is manifest in Japanese children now, promises a great deal; and I am rather optimistic about the future outcome. The Japanese are cut away from their moorings to the dead formalism, and real free thinking will take place in the Island Empire before long.

4. The rising tide of new Japanism, if I may call it so, means less consumption of foreign books. In the early days after the Restoration the Japanese students used English books as texts for all kinds of study. In my days we referred to foreign books for research.

Now the Japanese student can study any line of work without the help of foreign books, with the result that foreign languages occupy a smaller place in our education. What will come out of this I do not pretend to know.

The Japanese language was once considered an impossible one for foreigners to learn; but with the use of fewer and fewer Chinese characters it will become easier. If so, it might not be altogether a dream to conceive of the Westerner coming one step forward toward us and spending at least one twentieth or one fiftieth of his brain power in the study of the Japanese language. If there were twenty Americans in New York who could read Japanese, the greater part of the misunderstanding about Japan would disappear. Then they would know that there are a few things in Japan besides Mount Fuji and Cherry Blossoms. If they could only read a few poems of Japan they would cease to think that we are all laundrymen and strawberry pickers. Japanese words are very simple and if any of you have curiosity enough to take home a few examples I shall be delighted to give you some —

(Ohio — Nevada — Utah)

The story of the intellectual currents of one's country is never complete without a study of its imaginative literature. Then what is the modern literature of Japan which is forming the minds of the masses there? That is the subject I propose to discuss at my next lecture.

LECTURE IV

Modern Literature — The Novel, The Drama, and Poetry

I

In my last lecture I examined some outstanding traits of Japanese intellectual life, and surveyed journalism with special reference to its democratic tendencies. In this lecture to-day I propose to take up the story where I left it, and try to describe the subtler and more intimate side of Japanese life reflected in the imaginative literature of present-day Japan.

I long wondered why the Japanese were so little understood by the outside world. Then it dawned on me one day that it was to a great extent due to the fact that the more human side of our life was not presented to the outside world. We were mostly in touch with the great world through the channels of diplomacy, trade, and sometimes warfare. The daily lives of the common man and woman who laugh and weep, just as their brothers and sisters in the Western world, have not been revealed to the latter. Even in the days of Romanoff rule, the Russian people had a place in the sympathy and affection of Americans. The systems of government were a thousand miles apart in those days; yet Americans realized that Russian peasants were simple-hearted, human creatures, capable of love and joy and admiration, as Ruskin would say. And did this not come about mainly through the popularity of Russian literature in America? Through the works of Tolstoy, Turgenev, and Dostoevski, you were led to the firesides of Russian people; and you could not help liking the simple folk on the great plains of Northern Europe. But the contrary has been the case with us. Our two countries have stood in intimate, friendly relationship for a long time; yet the life of no country is less understood in America than that of Japan.

Nothing reveals the life of a people as much as its imaginative literature. If only we could present a Japanese " Huckleberry Finn " or a " Kim " to you, how Japanese boys would be endeared to the hearts of American boys. " Japanese literature must be presented to American audiences," I said to myself, walking along Fifth Avenue one autumn morning. Four years have passed since then. Nothing gives me greater pleasure, therefore, than having the rare privilege of presenting even a brief review of this very subject to such a distinguished audience to-day.

II

Art and literature have a peculiar position in Japanese life. Partly because of our temperament and partly by tradition, our daily routine is inseparably bound up with literature and art. The tea ceremony and flower arrangement occupy a secure place in the life of not only the aristocracy, but also the middle class. The education of a young woman is never complete without some lessons in poetry-writing. It is not uncommon to find a master of a grocery shop or a cobbler sending in his poem in competition for a prize offered by the local paper to which he subscribes. The New Year's number of all Japanese papers has a special feature every year. On that day is published the ten best poems selected by the poets laureate of Japan, to be read in the presence of the Emperor and his Court. The subject is given out a few months in advance each year, and thousands and thousands of people send in their poems. There is no qualification of class or standing, not even nationality. In fact, a few years ago Mrs. Burnett, an American lady, won the honor.

It is imaginative literature more than anything else that moulds the common opinions of a country. Literary criticisms, historical essays, as well as poems, novels, and dramas have a great influence in giving currency to ideas and direction to popular thinking. Moreover, it is the literary people who usually foreshadow coming changes. Japan is no exception to that general rule. In that respect, too, the modern literature of Japan is important, because what these poets and novelists think to-day, Japan will do to-morrow.

III

THE FIRST PERIOD

The development of the modern literature of Japan since the Restoration of 1868 can be divided into six periods. The first period covers the first seventeen years from 1868 to 1884. This we can call a dark period of the epoch of literary chaos, when the attention and energy of the whole nation were concentrated on the work of political and economic reconstruction. In those years of upheaval and commotion there was little place for literature. It was the age of the cult of the West. We made a frantic effort to catch up with the progress of the West after the seclusion of three long centuries. Everything Western was welcome. Things Eastern were thrown aside, and in some cases even destroyed. The same was true with literature. Nobody paid any attention to Japanese writings. The great literature of the Tokugawa era was buried deep in neglect, and translations of Western literature filled the book-shelves of the progressives. Political novels were in vogue and the works of Lord Lytton and Lord Beaconsfield had a wide circulation. A number of politicians wrote political fiction that had more popularity than literary merit. Only three things in the realm of the spirit are worthy of mention in this period. They are the introduction of English utilitarianism by Fukuzawa, the founder of Keio University; the spread of Christian teachings by Niijima, the founder of Doshisha University; and the propagation of the radical French philosophy by young men like Saionji, who is no other than the present serene conservative Genro, Prince Saionji. The first half of this period was marked by the ascendency of Anglo-Saxon literature, while the second half was characterized rather by zeal for French, German, and Russian literature.

Another feature of this epoch must be noted, namely, the simplification of the Japanese language itself. The ornate classical style of ancient times was superseded by the simpler form advocated by Fukuzawa and Nakamura. This, in turn, paved the way for the arrival of the second period of greater literary activities.

The Second Period

The year 1885 was a memorable year for two reasons. It was in that year that the famous writer, Shoyo, wrote his epoch-making essay on " The Essence of a Novel." As he was a great student of Shakespeare, I will call him " the Shakespearean." He made clear the function of the novel and laid down fundamental principles for the writers of Japan in their quest for a new form of literary expression. He criticized the morality novels of the old school, and laid stress on the need of a novelist's describing, with clear objectivity, the human life as such. He followed it up with a novel of his own, " The Life of Contemporary Students," which stirred a commotion among the literary people of those days. It opened the eyes of young men to a new type of writing; and Japanese literature took on a new color from this year.

It was also this year that gave birth to a society of writers called " Ken-yu-sha " or " The Association of Literary Friends," under the leadership of another great novelist, Koyo (or Maple Leaves). It was this group of novelists that, for ten years to come, was to stand at the forefront of literary activities and practically change the whole atmosphere of Japanese literature.

Koyo's (the Maple Leaves') great work, " The Confessions of Two Lovers — Two Nuns," appeared in 1889 and won him national recognition as one of the greatest writers of the day. His many other stories followed with equal success. His contribution to the literary world was threefold. He started a new school of fiction by setting an example in objective description. He also attracted the attention of the whole nation by making his stories especially entertaining, and thus created an atmosphere for future novelists. But his greatest contribution lay in the creation of a new style of prose — brilliant and ornate. He was, in fact, a master of our tongue; and by his conscientious and artistic skill he changed the style of writing, not only for fiction but also for the whole range of literature. His strength, however, was his weakness. He became so absorbed in style and in the merely interesting phases of stories that he neglected sincerity and penetration. He and his followers more or less played with their novels, and did not rise to the height of truly great writers.

In sharp contrast to Koyo (Maple Leaves) stood Rohan (as his greatest work was " The Pagoda," I will call him " The Author of The Pagoda "). The secret of his power was his indomitable idealism. His basic philosophy was Buddhism and he was more of a poet than a novelist. His place as a great writer was firmly established when he published his masterpiece, " The Pagoda," in 1895. It is the story of an architect who built a towering pagoda on new principles, in the face of tremendous opposition from his colleagues. A terrific storm rises on the day of completion and the huge structure is put to the severest of tests. The description of the raging storm and the architect standing at the very top of the pagoda ready to die in the ruin of his life work if fate so willed it, and the portrayal of the ultimate victory of the faith of the artist over the elements, are so vividly done that they occupy a lasting place in the prose of the past century.

The author of " The Pagoda," however, was not entirely free from the weakness of his age. His characters were types rather than individuals and his plots gave the impression that they were created by his imagination, not from the observation of real life. He lacked the receptive power of Koyo (Maple Leaves) and unlike him could not change his subjects with the changes that took place in the outside world. So his literary life came quickly to an end.

Besides these two great novelists there were two men of letters who laid the foundation for the new literature of Japan. One was Shoyo, the Shakespearean of whom I have already spoken, and the other was Ogai, a famous surgeon who wound up his life as the Surgeon General of the Army. As he was a great student of the German writer, Goethe, I will call him "Ogai, the student of Goethe." Shoyo, the Shakespearean, later became Professor of English Literature at Waseda University, and through his classroom have passed many of the present prominent writers of Japan. These two men were the guiding spirits of Japanese literature for more than forty years, and most of the progress in modern Japanese literature is due to them either directly or indirectly. It was fortunate for Japan that these two men differed fundamentally in sympathy, temperament, and culture. Shoyo, as I have said, was a student of Shakespeare; and his spirit was in harmony with Anglo-Saxon culture. He was very objective in his thinking and based his ideas on facts. He was moderate and well-balanced in style. In sharp contrast stood Ogai, the student of Goethe. He was devoted to German culture, particularly the writings of Goethe, and was fond of basing his arguments on concepts or theories of life and conduct. He was subjective and deductive while Shoyo was objective and inductive.

Their gifts were equally matched. They were both essayists, novelists, linguists, critics, dramatists, and poets. Their activities in the literary world were very long and diversified.

Ogai, the student of Goethe, commenced his literary activities in 1889 by writing three novels, all being the recollections of his student days in Germany. His earnest personality ran through the stories and this, along with his polished style, won him a place of first rank in the literary world. But the greatest contribution he made at this period was the part he played in a literary duel with Shoyo, the Shakespearean, on the correct attitude and function of a writer. This controversy infused a new spirit into the literary world, and raised many interesting points which were not even thought of by the writers of those days.

But perhaps the greatest achievement of this period, next to the novel-writing, was the introduction of a new tone in the dramas of Japan. The motive of this movement was more moral than artistic, but it revived a new interest in the stage and produced good results in many directions. In 1893 Shoyo, the Shakespearean, opened a new epoch by writing his famous " Essay on Historical Dramas," in which he laid down his own views on how to construct a play. He attacked the old dramas of Japan as " illusion plays," and emphasized the need of real plays with real characters. As was the case with him always, he followed this theory up with a play of his own, entitled " One Leaf of a Pau-

lownia." This was a play representing the last days
of the Toyotomis in the sixteenth century, with the
Osaka Castle as the scene of action. It marked the
dawn of a new era for the Japanese drama, even though
the actual staging of the play had a wait until the following period. During this period good translations of
real artistic value appeared. Futabatei Shimei, in a
sense greater than Koyo, introduced Russian novels
into Japan and wrote exquisite masterpieces of his
own, one of which, " The Adopted Husband," has been
translated into English. Historical writings also began
to flourish at the end of this period. Progress was not
confined, however, to prose-writing. There was a
marked stir among the poets, and young talents made
courageous efforts to start new movements, emancipat-
ing poetry from the dead hand of formalism. But
their hopes were to be realized in the next period by
the appearance of two great poets.

IV

THE THIRD PERIOD

The ten years that followed the Chinese-Japanese
War of 1894 were a great period for Modern Japan.
A new spirit that sprang from the consciousness of
power permeated the whole nation. Young Japan had
the first test of her modern equipments and came out
victorious, flushed with the vigor of a young man in
his twentieth year. The call of new adventure ran
through the blood and the note of glory rang in the
ears.

Japan found herself. The economic fabric of the

nation was undergoing a change, and new industrialism was fast taking root. Her place in the world rose over night. The new system of government seemed to be safely vindicated after the triumph over the great opponent. Everything seemed to promise a fair voyage ahead.

The reaction of the material world on the world of spirit was immense. The thirty years of zealous importation of Western culture began to bear fruit. The time had come for the Japanese to turn Western culture over in their minds, and to inquire resolutely into its significance for themselves.

The first outward sign of a turn of thought appeared in the rise of a new nationalism, distinct from the chauvinism of the preceding period. The spokesmen of this cult urged that the tradition of the past three thousand years must be respected, and that Western culture and foreign religions could serve the people only by conforming to traditional Japanism. Side by side with this nationalism there rose another cry — a cry for Cosmopolitanism, which laid emphasis on the position of Japan in the world. But these were the two different expressions of the same thing, the consciousness of a new Japan.

It was no wonder that at this period of military heroism literature took on a new note of hopefulness and individual expansion.

At the beginning of this period, the young and gifted writer, Takayama, wrote glowing essays on the theory of the superman expounded by the German philosopher, Nietzsche, and extolled the virtues of individualism, the merits of the superman, and the beauty and glory of life made manifest in the free expression of human instincts. These essays caught the imagination of the whole nation. They marked the death knell of the narrow moralism, formalism, and conventionalism inherited from old times. The spirit of Japan which had been waiting so long for emancipation from the bondage to feudal moralities, found at last a timely exponent in the daring young philosopher. A great stir was created among the literary people and a new period of romanticism was dramatically ushered in.

There was another and still more substantial reason for the prosperity of literature in this period. That was the material progress of the country after the war. Newspapers began to increase circulations, and innumerable magazines appeared in the market. Demands for literary productions increased in great proportion.

The first effect on imaginative literature appeared in the so-called "Concept Novel," which tried to interpret the conflicting theories of life that were growing up in the minds of people. This was decidedly a step forward from the former period, in that the novelists were becoming interested in the objective description of man in society. But the writers of this school did not produce any works of permanent value.

A second effect was to open the door to the novel of social criticism, and the first writer of this school was a young woman of delicate health and constrained material circumstances. Her pen name was Ichi-yo or "One Leaf." It fell to her lot to support her aged mother and a young sister. She determined to support them by her pen. When she was scarcely twenty she published her first novel. At the beginning of the

period under consideration, she rose to the very top of
the literary realm by producing works of real genius.
Exposed to the hardships of a selfish and heedless world
from her young childhood, her sensitive mind was over-
whelmed by the sad fate of mankind. In her first
novels, she revealed a spirit of impassioned revolt — the
revolt of womankind against the tyranny of society.
Above all did she resent the unjust treatment meted
out to women of the lower class. She saw no gleam of
hope or happiness for the daughters of the poor, and
the misery and melancholy of their life weighed heavily
on her spirit. Filled with sympathy for them, she challenged society with her fiery pen. Although her works
were far from perfect in literary form and finish, a new
note ran through them all. The intense earnestness and genuine enthusiasm of the great writer were
stamped on every page. There was nowhere to be
found a trace of the " playfulness " that characterized
the writers of the Koyo or " Maple Leaves " school.
In 1895 she wrote her great work, " Take-Kurabe,"
and her place in the literary history of Japan was established.

Her literary activities lasted only four years, for she
died in 1896 at the age of twenty-four. These four
short years are divided into two periods; and all her
stories of enduring power belong to the second period.
In the works of her last two years, the tone of impassioned revolt, which was uppermost in the first period,
was changed into that of quiet resignation. The sad
destiny of women everywhere, especially in the world
of the laboring poor, seemed so appalling that it was
beyond the power of weak mortals to defeat it by rebel-

lion. With painful sympathy she then began to draw objective pictures of women in poverty. Her style became less sentimental and artificial. As she was a poet by nature, her descriptions of misery were toned down with a poetic touch of beauty and restraint. In her "Thirteenth Night," meaning two nights before the full moon, there is a famous scene of two lovers meeting after years of separation. They had secretly loved in their childhood, but an unhappy marriage forced on the girl wrecked their lives. The girl was bound by law and convention to a rich and selfish husband. The boy, having squandered all his fortune through recklessness and despair, was driven to the necessity of pulling a "rickshaw" for a bare livelihood. After many years of separation and sorrow, they meet by chance on a moonlight night — the girl as the customer of the laborer. The young man, with a laconic simplicity, narrates the story of his life since their separation. The girl, listening with quiet eagerness, recalls to her mind the bygone days of secret joy and compares them with her present days of misery. Then at a tense moment she remembers her stern duty to her aged parents. The lovers part without a single sign betraying their inmost sentiments, and the dark curtain of silence is drawn over the pathetic scene. In a simple tale, simply told, in language of poetic beauty, the Japanese spirit of loyalty and unbending endurance is revealed.

The greatest work of this gifted authoress, "Take-Kurabe," which means "Comparing the Heights," is also a story of a boy and a girl torn asunder by fate. The boy is the adopted son of a Buddhist priest serving a temple near the Yoshiwara, and the girl is an adopted daughter of a house in that quarter. He is dedicated by his foster father to the religious life, and she by a curse of fortune to the gay life of a geisha. Yet they grow up through the sweet innocence of childhood without knowing what fate had prepared for them. The picture of their simple and joyful play is so sincerely and so beautifully drawn that it shines with living light. Upon a scene of almost holy loveliness steals at last the grim shadow of duty and the black curse of doom. The boy and girl bow before the decrees as the bamboo bows before the storm. He must go away from that place forever; and in the night before he goes, he leaves before the gate of his dear playmate a little pot of flowers. Early in the morning she finds it there. There the story abruptly ends, without describing what she did or even what she felt. The rest is left to the imagination of readers, another example of the fact that the essence of Japanese literature is suggestion and not expression.

Ichi-yo had that power so rare among even great artists, the power of revealing all that language holds, and leaving the immeasurable misery of genuine tragedy to the imagination of those who can walk serenely with Buddha or suffer with Jesus in the garden of Gethsemane. Thus in the writings of this true genius the imaginative literature of Japan made an immense gain. It was brought nearer to life. The terrible power of restraint was demonstrated in a manner never to be forgotten.

The year 1896, the year in which the pathetic life of this gifted woman came to an end, saw the appear-

ance of a great work by Koyo, the Maple Leaves. He
had long been a target of criticism and ridicule for not
producing any really great works, and as he was a sensitive man he felt it very keenly. Stung by the attacks,
he started early in 1896 to publish a long novel in a
Tokyo paper *Yomiuri*. " Tajo-Takon " or " Endless
Love, Endless Regrets," as he called it, was a masterpiece. It was a story of a disconsolate school teacher
whose days and nights were filled with memories of
his departed wife. The author's success in vividly
describing individual characters in the story is now considered as foreshadowing the coming period of naturalism in Japan. It was universally hailed as an achievement in the field of imaginative literature.

The next year he began to publish his most popular
novel " Konjiki-Yasha " or " The Demon in Gold Tis-
sue." With this novel, perhaps, the prose of the Meiji
era reached its height. It is a story of a young man
who is deceived by a woman, and devotes his whole life
to the accumulation of wealth in order to avenge himself. And he gets his revenge. The story vibrates with
dramatic interest and the characters described in it
come to life. It made a sensation in the reading world
and the praise of the author was on the lips of everybody. But as a work of literary value, it was below
the story he published the year before. He clearly
went one step down to capture the popularity of his
contemporaries. He was, however, successful in describing Japan in that period. It was the age of romanticism and people liked stories of unusual events
and unusual characters. Koyo died in 1903 at the age
of thirty-six, before he finished his last story. A num-

ber of writers attempted to finish this fragment, and even now every effort of a popular novelist to write a sequel appeals to the popular imagination. Koyo (Maple Leaves), with all his short-comings, was certainly one of the two or three greatest literary figures of the memorable era of Meiji. This period of romanticism was rather rich in successful novels, but I will refrain from confusing you by enumerating too many Japanese names. I will say only that the prose of modern Japan reached its high water mark in this period, as the writers were all bent on producing works of unquestioned literary skill. From the point of view of public interest they were unusually successful, because they turned out highly entertaining stories, thus widening the audience for novels. But their strength was their weakness. They gradually sank in literary value as they sought popularity. This inevitably brought about a tremendous reaction in the next period. But before we go into the transition in fiction we must give a glance at the field of poetry.

The study of Nietzscheism did not stop with mere criticism. The destructive period was always followed by a constructive one. The advocates of the superman theory themselves were not content with their own ideal. It did not satisfy the human spirit merely to glorify the life of natural instincts. So the followers of Nietzsche gradually turned in a new direction; and they became more and more religious. The gifted young critic, Takayama, cut himself away from the doctrines of Nietzscheism and devoted himself to the study of Buddhism, to which he had been converted. The tendency of the time gradually turned that way. Young men grew tired of scepticism and wanted to see light through religion. Many religious authors appeared, the foremost of whom was Ryosen, whose writings were acclaimed by young men. Romanticism reached its climax with the appearance of philosophic and religious writers like Takayama and Ryosen.

The age of romanticism is always the age of poetry, and Japan was no exception to the general rule. Poetry in all forms burst forth in this period.

In the August of 1897, an epoch-making book of poetry appeared. The author was a young teacher of a middle school in Sendai, a city two hundred miles north of Tokyo. For a number of years he had cast about for someone willing to publish his work, and at last he succeeded in selling all his poems for fifteen dollars cash without any royalty on them. He awoke one summer morning and found himself famous all over the country. The name of Toson, or " A Village of Wisterias," has become a household name. The book went into hundreds of editions and is still selling, much to the benefit of the publisher and publisher alone.

The popular form of Japanese verse had long been the short poem of either thirty-one or seventeen syllables. Toson (A Village of Wisterias) succeeded, by one master stroke, in giving Japan a new style of verse, a long poem with no limitation on the number of lines. In this freer form, the poets sang of the new spirit of Young Japan. The long-pent-up ferment among the young minds at last found an expression, in vivid, beautiful, and novel forms. The genuineness of sentiments, the earnestness of the spirit, and the beauty of the style, captured the imagination of the whole literary world. And there was an air of freedom over it all. The poet sang about nature, passionate love, and the glory of human endeavor.

Books by the same author followed in rapid succession with equal success, and the new form of poetry was firmly established. The sentimentalism of his first works was gradually toned down, and his broad interests gradually turned toward the dignity and beauty of creative labor. The flaming passion of youthful fire slowly died down to a deep and serene social sympathy. He emerged from the world of dreams into the domain of realities, which culminated in the production of great novels in the following period.

The spirit of innovation was not confined to the field of long poems. The art and form of the short poem was destined to undergo a revolution. In August, 1901, the literary world of Japan was to receive a great sensation. A collection of short poems entitled "Midare-gami," or "The Flowing Hair," was published, and all Japan gasped with admiration. It was the work of a young girl of twenty-two, who wrote under her real name "Aki-ko" or "The Child of a Gem." She later married a poet and is now known as Madam Yosano.

While the poems of Toson or "A Village of Wisterias" were under the influence of Western poets like Swinburne and Rossetti, the works of Aki-ko or "The Child of a Gem" were entirely Japanesque. She delved deeply into the classics of Japan and, while giving expression to the spirit of her age, used the old forms of her ancestors. Through her blood surged a torrent of romanticism and fearless passion. By bold lines on the love, tumult, and romance of human life, she shocked old-fashioned people and gave an unbounded joy to the young generation. She took immense delight in slighting the old formalities and narrow moralities. Her songs are full of bold denunciations of conventionalism. Her songs were soon on the lips of thousands. Her descriptive and imaginative poems are considered even better than her lyrical verses. She was particularly successful in singing about the beauty of Kyoto, the ancient capital of Japan where, ten centuries ago, centered the golden age of Japanese literature.

She is still living and holds her place at the forefront in the Japanese world of poetry. Her achievements have been truly remarkable, particularly when we remember that she has found time to write so many masterpieces and assume the motherly care of her ten children. Moreover, she has also distinguished herself in the woman's movement in Japan, as well as in the educational world.

Before I left Japan last July, I visited her at her home and among other things asked her to write a few verses for me. By the way, she has written eight thousand poems thus far. She took a pen and wrote me three, one of which I will try to give in a rough translation:

> Into the edifice which humanity
> has been building from
> time immemorial,
> I too drive a nail of gold.

Along with the awakening of the new spirit in poems embracing thirty-one syllables, there came another no less marked renaissance of Hokku or shorter poems of seventeen syllables. It was started by an unusual personality, Shiki, or " A Cuckoo," who combined in his person the qualifications of a great critic and the spirit of a creative genius. He started his movement by writing on the great poet Basho in 1893 and on Buson in 1896. His plea was " write poems of genuine objective and descriptive nature! " He commenced his work by first destroying the old-fashioned forms, and ended by constructing a school of poetry of his own. He and his followers practically ruled the whole field of Hokku. His influence also extended to the field of prose. His plea for pure, objective description untrammeled by subjective views, opened a new gate for Japan's prose writers. He thus paved the way for the arrival of the period of naturalism. Shiki was most active in the years 1898 and 1899. Unhappily, nature did not favor him with a strong physique, and he had to spend most of his later years in bed, dying in 1902.

A marked progress was noticed in this period in the field of drama. Better dramas of literary value were written and staged. But we cannot tarry too long in the period of romanticism, as a still more important period is coming soon.

LECTURE V

Modern Literature — The Novel, The Drama, and Poetry (Continued)

V

The Fourth Period

Some critics think that the modern literature of Japan, in its strict sense, begins with the rise of naturalism immediately after the Russo-Japanese War of 1904–1905; and I am inclined to agree with them.

The ten years that preceded the Russo-Japanese War was the age of great expectations. The whole nation was united in the single motive, and all the energy of the people was bent on the attainment of the one object. The humiliation of the intervention by Russia, Germany, and France, at the end of the Sino-Japanese War went deep into the minds of the Japanese. The high-handed manner in which those three powers ordered Japan out of Port Arthur, which she had won after a hard fight, opened the eyes of the people. They realized that they were weak. They realized also that another test of might, this time with a European Power, was inevitable. The humiliation united the whole people. Their life was permeated by the thought of that one object. The heroic endeavor on which the whole nation was bent gave rise to the period of romanticism in literature.

But what was the result of the Russo-Japanese War? Did the result justify the preparatory endeavor, and the stupendous sacrifices made during the war? There were unmistakable signs of disappointment throughout the country. There arose a serious doubt about the romantic glory of nationalism. In the wake of national exhaustion crept in a new spirit, the spirit of scientific realism.

The natural sciences of the West were training the minds of the Japanese for analytical and critical enterprises. The scientific spirit craves the truth, the ruthless truth at whatever cost. It mercilessly strips from the mind the sentimental veil of romanticism. Japan had lived too long in the realm of romanticism, and the romantic dream reached the climax in the Russo-Japanese War. The scales dropped from her eyes and Japan looked at the world with a new understanding.

The literary people are always ahead of others in reading the changing spirit of the times. So it was the Japanese writers who first grasped the meaning of the scientific age that was dawning upon Japan. The whole business, in a nutshell, meant naturalism in literature.

The rise of naturalism is a very significant event; not only in the history of literature, but also in the whole history of the Japanese people. Young Japan emerged from the dreamland of color prints and the myth of the Sun Goddess, and stood face to face with the naked truth of the world in which she lived.

The atmosphere that surrounded the Japanese seemed entirely unbearable. Romanticism was a broad day dream; idealism and religion were sheer sentimentalism; and the old moralities were sheer hypocrisy. Everything was false. It must go. So with deadly earnestness, they started to pull down all the existing theories and ideas. They were intent on destruction and exposition.

An able writer returned home at this time from his study in Europe, and rose at once to the forefront of the movement. This writer was Hogetsu, or " To embrace the moon," who began in 1905 untiring activities in both the critical and creative spheres. His promising life was later clouded by a love affair with a leading actress for whom he wrote a number of plays. His unhappy career ended in 1919 by his death from Spanish influenza. A month later, the actress stirred the land by committing suicide in a most dramatic fashion. But that is not a story with which we are concerned here.

Hogetsu (To embrace the moon) and his friends carried all Japan before them. Naturalism overran the whole country.

Before we go into the study of literary works of this period, let us briefly survey the ground and find out the reasons for the change. We can count four main causes that were responsible for the new turn in the realm of letters.

The first and the most important cause was the ascendency of scientific spirit, owing to the failure of romanticism to satisfy the human quest for knowledge about life.

The second was " the sadness of victory " experienced after the war with Russia.

The third was the introduction of continental literature in place of English.

The fourth was the importation of the philosophy of Pragmatism.

The writer who really ushered in the new period was Doppo, or "A Lone Walker." He, true to his pen-name, was a lone traveler in the vale of life. A man of considerable genius and sincerity, he looked at the human scene with strange eyes. In an age of romanticism, he did not hesitate to write about the brutal truth and the stark realities of life with a penetrating pen. His works, however, were at first unpopular in the age of Koyo (the Maple Leaves), when people liked gorgeous style and entertaining stories. In 1897 he wrote his story "Uncle Gen," but nobody paid any attention to him. Then he wrote his monumental work, "The Field of Musashi" in 1901, but still he was unnoticed. Even the famous "Beef and Potatoes" received no recognition in the same year. In these dark days of obscurity, he was suffering from an unfortunate love affair, which he put down in his "A Chronicle That Does Not Lie," a work of singular insight and transparent sincerity. He was too far ahead of the time.

With the advent of naturalism, however, came his days of recognition and triumph. In 1905 his "Collection of Short Stories" was received by the public with enthusiasm; and from that day on, his sovereignty was unchallenged. He rose at once to the summit of Mount Parnassus. But the days of glory did not last very long for him. The long years of poverty and hardship had undermined his health; and he died in 1907, quite a young man of thirty-six.

Doppo was a born poet. From his childhood he looked at the world with an original mind. The thing that impressed him most was the sadness of the life of the multitude. He wrote in his " A Chronicle That Does Not Lie," " It is not difficult to understand the meaning of the lives of great men and philosophers. They have all had ideals and have run through their seven lives filled with great and sublime hopes. By looking at their ideals, you can understand the meaning of their lives. But what can we say of the lives of the great multitude of men! What meaning is there to their poor, simple annals? We stand simply aghast at the tragic sight. Is it not this gloomy truth that has driven many wise and good men into pessimism? Yes, is this not the origin of religions? " In this vein he was constantly thinking of the fate of the masses, and so a deep note of melancholy ran through his writings. In the end he arrived at the stern fatalism of Mark Twain.

Doppo stood in sharp contrast to Koyo (the Maple Leaves) for whom life was pleasure, and literature a delight. Koyo was one of the few fortunate people of the world who find happiness shining everywhere. Doppo (A Lone Walker) grieved over life with the mass of humanity. His own mortal life was short and sad, but his works of art will last as long as the Japanese language endures.

A few minutes ago I spoke of a poet by the name of Toson, or " A Village of Wisterias," who in 1898 introduced a new form of poetry into Japanese literature. After a silence of about six years, he came back into the scene, this time as a novelist. In 1906 he published a long novel called " Hakai," or " The Breaking of the Pledge." As was the case with his first poems, this story created a sensation in the literary world. It was a new novel of naturalism. It was a tale of a school teacher who belonged to the class of outcasts. He gave a pledge to his father never to reveal his origin, as it would mean the end of all his hopes for a career and a high position in the world of learning. It meant more than that; it meant the loss of a sweetheart dearer than life. He later came under the influence of a leader who had valiantly declared his origin and faced the persecution that followed the revelation. The teacher then spent weeks and months in agony debating with himself whether to keep or break the pledge made to the soul of his departed father. The suffering of the man and the hard social world of respectability in which he labored to maintain a position are realistically described. At the end of the story he bravely declares his origin, surrenders everything dear to him, and leaves his native land forever.

In this novel, the author exposed to the world a painful side of the Japanese life, the existence of a social injustice demanding a remedy. It was not only realistic; it was beautifully written. The famous critic Hogetsu, or " To embrace the moon," praised it with unreserved admiration, and said, " This story shows us that the Japanese literary world has arrived at a turning point. The spirit of the problem novel of the modern naturalist writers of Europe has for the first time found an equal and worthy expression in our world of fiction."

In 1908, Toson wrote " The Spring "; and in 1910, he published " The House," and firmly established his place in Japanese letters. A critic called him the Turgenev of Japan. At all events, he resembles the Russian novelist in the sense that he combines in himself the sensibilities of the poet and the analytical powers of the realist. Both described actual life in a plain, lucid style and grasped its realities, but always supplemented this description with the expression of genuine sentiment. Toson's style is a model of Japanese prose, and I make bold to say that in him the prose of the Meiji era reached its highest finish. As a man, he is very simple and modest. Like Anatole France he is a painstaking writer; and all his paragraphs, although they look very simple at first sight, are in fact chiseled with extreme care.

He went to France during the war; and on his return published a novel, "A New Life," courageously exposing a mistake in his own past. With that his major activities ceased, and he rarely writes now.

There are a few other authors of no small consequence who belong to this period. In fact the age of naturalism was very rich in works of decided merit. The names of Katai, Shusei, and Hakucho must not be left unmentioned. These men all turned their searchlights on the darker sides of human life and mercilessly exposed them. They were shockingly realistic. Customs, habits, and institutions that the writers of the past ignored with polite avoidance, they squarely faced. "Description of real life and no artistic style" was their slogan. They consciously strove for simplicity — even for crudity. They ignored the subtle moralities and discussed the problems of sex with startling frankness. In this they represented a reaction from the sickly romanticism of the preceding period. Truth they put before beauty, and then contended that in life there was more sordidness than high delight. So " the more sordid, the truer the description," became their cry. They also revolted against systematic idealism and laid stress on the theory that chaos is the natural, the true state of the Universe. They therefore left every problem unsolved. Even an attempt at a solution of anything seemed to them following a delusion and not reality. They ridiculed every kind of a positive concept of life and duty, and dwelt in what they called " the world of facts " — facts with no coördinating relation between them.

Thus naturalism was a great success in the first stage of destruction and exposition. It exposed the weakness of romanticism and shallow idealism, and exposed the hypocrisy of conventional moralities. It drove narrow-minded tradition and many falsehoods from the realm of literature. It taught the nation to look at things with the fearless eye of scientific research, and raised the standard of novel writing from the domain of playthings to the plane of serious human endeavor.

But after ten years of naturalism, Japan began to suffer from an excess of it. It destroyed the past beliefs and idealism but constructed nothing in their stead. It emphasized chaos, but human minds are never long happy in chaos. Living in this atmosphere of brutal scepticism, people began to pine for a world where they could attain some peace of mind. They got tired of the everlasting realities and yearned for a gleam of light, idealism, and hope. Thus came the inevitable quest for a new idea, and it too bore fruit in time.

VI

THE FIFTH PERIOD

Naturalism was on the ebb in 1909 and was dead in 1912, when a new tide of fresh idealism set in; but there was a curious feature which should not escape our attention, i.e., that in the latter days of naturalism there was an independent current running alongside the main stream. Through those days there was one great writer and thinker whom the surging tide of realism could not submerge. It was Soseki Natsume, the George Meredith of Japan.

He occupied a chair which had been left vacant by the death of Lafcadio Hearn, and was quietly teaching English at the Imperial University of Tokyo. In 1905 he began to contribute to a magazine a novel in serial form. It had a curious title: " I am a Cat." It was supposed to be the impression on a cat of human life around him. It was a detached picture of the contemporary age with a vein of genuine humor running throughout the story. It was at the end of the sad war with Russia and people were longing for the sound of laughter. So the story at once caught the popular imagination and the author was no longer a teacher but a leading novelist.

His tale had no particular plot. It had neither beginning nor end. Every part of it was interesting and independent from the others. Readers waited with impatience for the appearance of the next issue of the magazine; and he was made to continue the series by the publisher, apparently against his will. He complained of it often. I was one of his students. He used to come to the class and say, "I am going to murder the cat one of these days," and finally he did. All of a sudden he made the cat of his famous story drink beer from a glass left by the master, drop in a water bucket, and sing out in a most hilarious way, revealing all sorts of cheerful things he saw in the water. And that was the end of the cat. The public was disappointed, but could not complain about the delightful manner in which he killed the cat and ended the story.

In 1906 he wrote his long novel called "The Pillow of Grass," which is a Japanese idiomatic expression of travel. He remarked that the difference between a picture and a novel was said to lie in the fact that whereas the former had only the space element, the latter had the time element as well. And, he contended, if according to Lessing's "Laokoön," time can be put into a picture, there is no reason why it cannot be suppressed in a novel. So he wrote this novel without any development through a lapse of time, in other words with no time element at all. It was a beautiful story which, although highly interesting, contains no element of development. He puts into it a great deal of his philosophy.

Natsume was a great scholar and a thinker. He had a profound knowledge of Chinese classics, and assiduously studied English literature. He was one of the friends of Shiki (The Cuckoo) who revived Hokku or shorter poems, and was a poet of that school. During his three years' stay in London, he began to doubt whether "literature" meant the same thing in the East and the West. He collected necessary data and on his return published an essay of over five hundred

pages called "On Literature," in which he explained
the difference between the conceptions of the two
civilizations. In illustrating his theory, in a number
of places, he employed verses in three different languages, English, Chinese, and Japanese, and thus
brought out the difference in sentiment and underlying concepts.

With all his knowledge of English literature he was
entirely Oriental in mentality, taste, and philosophy.
His basic idea was Buddhism. In the heyday of naturalism, he was not afraid of professing his own idealism. He taunted the exponents of naturalism, saying,
"They contend that their works deal with fundamentals alone. But what are the fundamentals? Theirs are
fundamentals only when viewed in our narrow sphere
of life and death. If man's outlook on life is confined
to that sphere, the realities of the naturalists may indeed be absolute fundamentals. But suppose one
could batter down the portals of our visible life and
death and reach the world beyond it, who can tell
then whether their so-called 'fundamentals' might not
sink down to the level of secondary affairs?"

In his Buddhistic mind he could not conceive the
life of flesh as the only substantial thing worthy of
contemplation. In his conception he was a thorough
Japanese of the old school. He was dramatically op-
posed to the naturalist theory of life. All through his
works that antagonism is expressed. He stood like a
rock of Gibraltar against the beating tide of naturalism, and around him there grew up a group of writers
who later became the leaders in the school of new
idealism.

Soseki was very prolific; and in the twelve years of his literary activities he wrote over fifteen long novels and innumerable short stories and essays. They are all masterpieces of Japanese literature and will no doubt live forever as true expressions of the culture of Japan at the beginning of the twentieth century.

Soseki's attitude toward literature was carefully explained in a very interesting essay called " A Loitering Taste." In this, he said, " Life abounds in all kinds of leisure. To comment on the quality of tea, to water flowers in the garden, to dally with pictures and sculptures, or to make a few jokes, these are all little delights of idle moments in life. There is no reason why these also should not be material for literature. The loitering taste is the taste for quietly lingering at every pleasant or interesting spot as long as possible. It is therefore a taste that does not make for rapid development in a story. In other words, it is the taste that only a man who is not hurried in his mind can enjoy. A man of this way of life, for instance, goes shopping. He is sure to tarry on his way. He will stop in front of a police box to watch a boy who is delivering a rat to a policeman, he will also stop to listen to the tale that an unknown braggart is telling his friends. Thus the unhurried shopper moves slowly on his way. To a busy man this can never happen. He is out for shopping, so he must shop with grim determination. When the shopping is over, his work is over too. The same is true in a novel. If the writer's whole passion is centered on fate and, particularly, the fate of the hero in the story, he has no genial ease of mind; and, accordingly, there is in his work no art of leisure."

There was some element of true greatness in Soseki. He had a reasoned religion and a high moral sense. In the age of realistic naturalism, he summoned the young generation to a life of truer perspective and nobler service. He was a master of arts. His prose in lucidity and restrained power was peerless in his time. And his humor! It was telling. He was poetic. To read his work after the sordid and realistic writings of the naturalist school was like breathing fresh air after a long ride in a rush-hour subway car. He was particularly strong in the minute psychological analysis of characters. Although he was compared to George Meredith because of the depth of his thought, he wielded far more influence on his nation than did Meredith on England, owing to his lucidity of style.

Another phase of the reaction against naturalism, an over-emphasis of crude reality — took the form of extolling beauty to an exaggerated extent. It was called "neo-romanticism" and tended to epicureanism. The works of Kafu who wrote "A Sneer," in 1910, and those of Tanizaki, who published "Satan," "Totoo," "A Boy," and others, about the same time, are typical of this school. Tanizaki is still a young man and is often compared to Oscar Wilde.

The philosophy of pragmatism was now being replaced in popular favor by the teachings of Bergson and Eucken. The literary world of Japan was turning from naturalism to idealism.

In 1910 a new magazine called *The White Birch* appeared. It was a monthly edited by a group of students, mostly scions of the aristocracy, whose living was secure and who wrote for the love of the art, not for bread. Nobody paid them much attention at first, but their work had a germ that was destined to live and grow. They sought in pure disinterestedness for new values. They had youth, they had leisure, and they had sincerity. A combination of these qualities had never failed and they did not now fail. Slowly they attracted the attention of the literary world; and by 1916 they developed a distinct school of novelists, exponents of the new idealism.

When naturalism was spending its force in 1912, the young writers of *The White Birch* gradually gained in literary fame. Takero Arishima, the Tolstoyan, one of the most prominent among them, caught and held the attention of the whole country by his "The Laboratory," "The Daybreak," "The Labyrinth," and other stories published in 1916 and 1917. In these early novels he wrote about his life in America, where he had spent years as a student. His drama "Before and After Her Death" is a vivid description of his wife's death and his "To My Young Ones" is a short story addressed to his three sons, telling about their mother. From 1920 on, he was one of two or three authors who swayed the thought of the majority of young people in Japan. His novel "A Woman" made perhaps the widest appeal. All his novels — more than twenty in number — which he published in serial form, sold by the thousand, sometimes reaching the high mark of sixty or seventy thousand.

Arishima was an ardent admirer of Walt Whitman, and organized a literary society called "The Society of the Leaves of Grass." He also translated Whitman's poems into Japanese. He was also a great ad-

mirer of Tolstoy and liked the great Russian, and wrote
and talked of the power of love and affection to cure
the ills of a world sick with strife and bitterness. He,
like Tolstoy, had immense sympathy for all who labored in poverty. The fortune he inherited from his
father became a burden for him, and so he gave it all
up in 1922. His estate in the Northern island of Hok-
kaido, he turned over to the tenants with a quiet gesture of relief. His beautiful house in Tokyo as well
as his shares in the prosperous N. Y. K. or Japan Mail
Steamship Company, he decided to give to the work
of labor education. He himself lived the simple life
described by Tolstoy in his " Resurrection." He was at
the very summit of his power when his unfortunate
love affair ended his life in 1923, in a dramatic manner
that created a commotion in the whole country. He
was just over forty when he died. His work lives after
him, feeding the currents of humanitarian idealism in
an age weary of the sordid realism of the naturalism
school.

In the same group with Arishima we may place another writer who is still at work in the sphere of human
idealism: namely, Saneatsu Mushakoji. He is under
forty and is yet in the process of development, so that
it is too soon to pass a final judgment on him and his
literary merit. He has written thus far a number of
novels and short stories. He is particularly fond of
expressing his ideas in dramatic form. Last year he
published a long story called " A Certain Man," which
is in fact his autobiography and can be well compared
with Doppo's, " A Chronicle That Does Not Lie." In
" A Certain Man," the reader is led frankly and sin-

cerely into the story of the growth and inner struggles
of an original and philosophic mind. Mushakoji is also
an exponent of the gospel of love as the best hope for
the searchers after truth. He is under the spell of
Tolstoy, Buddha, and Christ. Quotations from these
teachers, and their interpretations of life, are frequently met in his novels and dramas.

About ten years ago he made up his mind to carry
out his fundamental ideas in a scheme of life, and accordingly he started a new village along communistic
lines. His "new village" attracted the attention of
the whole country and he is still living there with his
friends. How his literary genius will develop in this
fixed form of social economy is an interesting thing to
watch.

In 1916 another spokesman of the new idealism, a
young man under thirty, wrote a drama called "The
Priest and his Disciples." It at once attracted the attention of the reading public and went into two hundred editions in a few years. The author's name is
Kurata and his work is a Christian interpretation of
the life of the famous Buddhist priest, Shinyan. It is a
fascinating story and gave great stimulus to the ideal-
istic trend in Japanese literature. There are many
other writers worth mentioning, but time does not allow me to dwell too long on the latest phase of our
literary life.

In conclusion, we may say, what of the future? A
few years prior to his death, Arishima, the Tolstoyan,
wrote an article on "The New Literature of the Proletariat," in which he contended that the conception
of literature heretofore prevailing has been a bourgeois

conception, and that it is coming to a close with the approaching end of the bourgeois rule. Therefore, he went on to say, the new literature of the proletariat will appear in time and that can be written only by the sons and daughters of the proletariat. It followed, he continued, that the only thing which a man like himself, born in a bourgeois family, could do was to help usher in the new age of proletarian literature.

Arishima's declaration of faith as to the future was the beginning of a controversy in the literary world. Young writers began to attack all the popular novelists, on the ground that they were mere bourgeois who had no message for the new world of labor about to take the place of the old order. Meanwhile Japan waited to see these young critics, born and reared in the laboring class, prove their theory by producing literature of unquestioned artistic value fated to endure. Whether they can do it or not, remains for coming days to reveal. For the present, the literary world of Japan is ruled by two main schools of writers. One of them is the school of new idealism, in its many forms, but always benign, humane, and looking to a nobler tomorrow. The other is composed of the surviving naturalists, but they differ from the old artists of that persuasion in that they cannot confine their works to crude, descriptive realism, but are impelled by the Zeitgeist to reckon with the choices or problems set by fate. For the present the gamut seems to have been run, or, to use another figure, the pendulum seems forced to swing within definite limits. Will some new planet, hitherto undreamt of, appear within our ken? Who dares make answer?

LECTURE VI

The Impact of The American Immigration Law on Japanese Life

To gather up again the threads of my argument, I may briefly summarize my previous lectures. In the first place, I showed that the restoration in Japan was not a revolution but a triumph of feudal forces, and that the germs of liberalism that appeared in that epoch were trampled down under two foreign wars and vigorous foreign policies. In my second lecture, there was outlined the rise of a new liberal movement after the outbreak of the Great War in Europe — a liberal movement that was fortified by a growing middle class, and that found expression in many ways, notably in a juster policy toward China and Korea and the announcement of a manhood suffrage bill. The third lecture was devoted to a survey of the labor movement that swung rapidly at first toward syndicalism and violence and then, relieved of many severe police restrictions under liberal influences, promised coöperation with liberal leaders in the interest of domestic reform and international amity. Now I have come to a consideration of the so-called "immigration question," in its relation to the evolution of social forces in Japan and their eventual pressure upon the world relations of Japan.

In order to explain Japanese sentiment on this matter, it is necessary to point out that for more than half a century Japan has looked upon America as a kind of elder brother, both in the development of her domestic affairs and in her dealings with other nations. For more than half a century Japan has looked to America for friendly advice and help, and has met at every turn good will and material assistance. Let me enumerate some of the great debts which Japan owes to America.

First of all, the educational system of Japan, which makes the Japanese nation the only literate nation in the Orient, was modelled on the American plan. The Japanese minister of education, Viscount Mori, who laid the foundations of our system, had been a minister to Washington and had learned to admire the public school system of America. On his return, he devoted himself to convincing his countrymen that they should follow the example set by your country. Moreover, in the working out of the plan, the Japanese Government had the counsel of an American, David Murray, whose name will be celebrated forever in the annals of our intellectual life.

In the next place, Japan owes largely to American influence her escape from one of the most deadly curses of the Orient; namely, the opium habit. Shortly before I left Japan, I had a long talk with a noted statesman, now a privy councillor, who told me an amazing story about this stroke of good fortune for our country. I may use his language: " We owe a deep debt to America, one that we can never forget. In the first commercial treaty with America, a provision was inserted, on American recommendations, prohibiting the opium traffic. If that step had not been taken then, it is hardly probable that Japan would have been able to stop that dreadful traffic. When it was taken, Japan had a significant precedent to which she could point in her dealings with other foreign countries. But Japan narrowly avoided this awful peril. About fifty years ago " — continued the old statesman — " when Mr. Kohei Kanda was leaving his post as governor of Kobe, a great banquet was tendered him by the foreign residents in that city, and I acted as the translator on that occasion. In the course of his speech expressing his thanks for the honors accorded to him, Mr. Kanda said: 'We Japanese are deeply indebted to America for the suggestion that the prohibition of the opium trade be inserted in all treaties with foreign powers. If that noble precedent had not been set by America, Japan would have been cursed with the opium traffic as China has been cursed by it.' This statement by the governor made a tremendous sensation among the foreigners present and the citizens of a certain nationality cried out, No! No! As a young man," concluded the venerable statesman, " I was profoundly moved by that incident, and I have cherished my gratitude to America for her service to us all through the intervening years." Whenever a Japanese gives thanks that his country has escaped the ravages of that terrible drug, he must remember the services of America more than half a century ago. This prohibition of the importation of opium is in Article 4, Clause 3, of the first American-Japanese Treaty of 1858.

It is to America also that Japan owes her prison reform, which did away with so many cruelties of the ancient penal system. In the application of humane sentiments in this important sphere, Japan is under everlasting obligations to Dr. John C. Berry, a Christian missionary of the early days.

Indeed I must say that the debt of Japan to American missionaries is manifold and heavy. I shall not speak of controversial religious questions, for that would not be appropriate to this occasion; but it is just to record here that American missionaries have made significant contributions to the development of every phase of humane and liberal movements in Japan — to the advancement of social work in all its aspects, to the emancipation of Japanese women from ancient wrongs, to the improvement of our economic life. If you will take the outstanding figures in nearly every field of beneficent work in Japan, you will find men and women who in their early life came under the influence of American missionaries. The first foreigners whom the Japanese took into their homes and learned to know intimately were American missionaries through whose faces and lives shone the gentle spirit of Jesus Christ. Not long ago, when I told an American woman that thousands of Japanese early learned to think of Christian teachings as the law of American life, she shot back at me the reply: "Well, you had no business taking the missionaries so seriously!" Perhaps not, but we did; and that fact entered deeply into the psychology of the Japanese people in their thinking about America.

In the field of diplomacy, also, Japan learned to look upon America as no hard taskmaster bent upon obtaining the pound of flesh in every controversy. In the more than fifty years of our diplomatic relations, not a single angry controversy marred our discussions and conclusions. That is not all. America on more than one occasion went out of her way to do a generous act not required by the amenities followed by the powers of the world in general. For example, some years after a fine of $3,000,000 was laid upon Japan for the Shimonoseki incident of 1863 by the four foreign powers involved, the Congress of the United States returned the American share of the indemnity in a magnificent gesture of generosity, and the money was used in improving the harbor of Yokohama. When it looked as if certain European powers might intervene in the Russo-Japanese War in an unfriendly manner, President Roosevelt undertook to hold the scales of justice even as between the two belligerents. In taking the action that he did, he followed all the proper canons of neutrality, but at that time fair neutrality was benevolence to Japan.

Nor in recent times have our diplomatic relations departed in spirit from older precedents. When Japan fulfilled an obligation of justice in returning Tsingtao to China, the desire for American approval and continued American friendship was a powerful element in bringing about the surrender of territory bought by Japanese blood. When Japan surrendered the Anglo-Japanese alliance, entered the Washington Conference, and accepted a sixty per cent navy, the desire for American friendship was always uppermost in the minds of our people. When Japan devoted her remaining share of the Boxer indemnity to educational work in China, she was not oblivious to the American example and the effect of her action upon American sentiment. Such is the background of our historic relations. Such were the sentiments of the Japanese people when the sudden crash of the closing door came ringing in our ears.

I come now to the most delicate subject of my lectures, namely the relation of the recent immigration act to the interplay of the social forces in Japan which I have just outlined. The task is difficult, and it would be easier to close with the usual diplomatic amenities. But taking seriously the obligations resting upon me here, I feel bound to present to you as accurately as I can, without the slightest trace of complaint or bitterness, the attitude of those who are working for the development of a liberal Japan.

First of all, let us bring together the salient facts in this controversy. When friendly relations were first established between the United States and Japan, the gates of America were wide open to immigrants from all parts of the world. In 1864, the party of Abraham Lincoln called America " the asylum of the oppressed of all nations " and declared that immigration " should be fostered and encouraged by a liberal and just policy." Capitalists on the western coast, especially the railway builders, welcomed Chinese laborers; and later, Japanese began to come across to these hospitable shores. The significant fact in this connection is that in the early days of our relations, the Japanese people grew accustomed to associating friendship with America and the cordial welcome accorded to Japanese immigrants.

When in the course of time, there arose, as the result of many forces which it is unprofitable to discuss, serious friction on the Pacific Coast, the Government of the United States and the Government of Japan entered into the famous Gentlemen's Agreement of 1907, by which the latter undertook to restrain the migration of Japanese laborers. It has been claimed that the said agreement was not a treaty, and had no high constitutional sanction. Still the Japanese people looked upon it as a solemn international understanding; and if I am not mistaken, executive agreements are recognized in government practice and the treatises of publicists as binding in law and conscience. At all events, to use the language of Professor Treat, " the Japanese understood that as long as they kept their part of the agreement, the United States would not pass an exclusion law against the Japanese." This impression was confirmed in 1911 when, during the revision of the treaty of 1894, the provision declaring the right of the United States to regulate the immigration of laborers was omitted from the new text, on the understanding that the Japanese ambassador again declared the intention of his Government to maintain with equal effectiveness the control that it had been exercising over the migration of laborers. Our impression was again strengthened when we read in Mr. Roosevelt's Autobiography that the abrogation of the treaty would be necessary if the United States ever undertook to exercise the right of exclusion. It has been said that Mr. Roosevelt was unwise, from the American point of view, in making the Gentlemen's Agreement; and that Mr. Taft was equally unwise in negotiating the treaty of 1911. But there they stood, and the people of Japan looked upon them as understandings to be loyally kept.

But it has been alleged that Japan did not live up honorably to the terms of that Agreement. That was a matter of fact to be ascertained by an official inquiry, and to the best of my knowledge and belief, neither the executive nor the legislative branch of the government of the United States has ever made a scientific and searching inquiry into this allegation. Still, the passage of the immigration act carried with it the implication that the Congress of the United States, to say the least, suspected the integrity of the Japanese Government, as far as the discharge of all obligations arising under the Agreement was concerned. It may be that Congress entertained no such idea; but the methods by which the act was passed, rightly or wrongly, gave that impression to Japan.

It has been said that President Roosevelt had no power to bind the Congress of the United States not to pass an exclusion act. Nobody in Japan doubts or questions the constitutional and legal and sovereign right of Congress to enact such a law. It was not a question of power, but of action in view of certain circumstances and certain outstanding agreements. I beg to refer the lawyers to the logic and spirit of Edmund Burke's immortal speech on " Conciliation with America." Surely the Japanese people will be pardoned if they are unable to appreciate the legal argument and are prone to fix their eyes upon the Agreement.

It has been said that the issue at stake, the supreme

issue before Congress, was the protection of American civilization against a flood of Japanese immigrants. With all due respect, I beg to dissent from that contention. No responsible person in Japan has ever desired, or now desires, to force upon the United States any class of immigrants that was not wanted. No intelligent person in Japan looked upon the United States as an outlet for a redundant population. I venture the assertion that the right of any number or class of Japanese to migrate to America was no part whatever of the issue there. The issue in Japan was whether the Japanese nation was to stand on an equal footing with Western powers, or to be cut off from the fellowship and be driven back upon a purely Oriental policy and theatre of operation.

The methods pursued by Congress in passing the Immigration Act were even more significant than the substance of the Act. When, nearly half a century ago, Congress passed the first Chinese exclusion act, President Hayes vetoed the bill and suggested, instead of hasty and drastic action on the part of the United States, a friendly conference with the Government at Peking, remarking in his veto message: " This ancient Government, ruling a polite and sensitive people, distinguished by a high sense of national pride, may properly desire an adjustment of their relations with us which would in all things confirm and in no way endanger the permanent peace and amity and growing commerce and prosperity which it has been the object and effort of our existing treaties to cherish and perpetuate." So a commission of distinguished American citizens was sent to Peking and in due course concluded a treaty sanctioning the limitation and suspension of Chinese immigration to America, the United States to be the judge of the degree of necessity. The Japanese exclusion bill, on the other hand, paid no such deference to the partner affected by the action. Without any preliminary ceremonies, Congress brushed aside with a magnificent gesture an Agreement which Japan was endeavoring to fulfill, and slammed the door in the face of the Japanese nation, even of those Japanese who may wish to come here for a year or two to search out the excellent features of your civilization and commerce. Is it strange that the impression created in Japan by this action was painful, even admitting that Congress was entirely within its legal rights?

By a curious coincidence, the Immigration Act broke in upon the meditations of the Japanese people at a moment when the nation was bleeding from the wounds inflicted by the greatest calamity ever visited upon mankind by earthquake and fire. A tremendous amount of the national capital lay in utter ruin, more than two hundred thousand people had been killed by falling buildings or burnt to death in a raging whirlwind of fire, industries were prostrate, vast regions devastated, and national economy subjected to awful strains at every point. In the midst of our afflictions, the nation that had literally shaken open our gate, introduced us to the family of nations, sent Christian missionaries to teach us the ways of brotherhood and peace, and given us friendly counsel and advice at every turn, waived aside a long-standing agreement with us and slammed its own gate shut in our face.

It may be said that all this is mere sentiment. That is true. But sentiment is one of the great forces in the world with which statesmen must reckon.

So I may summarize that immigration in itself was not a substantial element in the issue raised by the act of Congress, but that the methods by which the bill was passed and the circumstances amid which it was written upon the statute books, produced a profound and widespread impression throughout the length and breadth of Japan and brought in its train grave consequences. This does not mean, to repeat what I have already said, that any intelligent Japanese thinks for a moment of waging war upon America over a matter that is fundamentally domestic in character. It does not mean that the Japanese are going to boycott American goods on any large scale, or strike at commerce between the two nations, or seek to disturb the existing friendly relations between the two governments. It does mean that an explosive force has been lodged in the Japanese mind — an explosive force that those who seek ways of international peace and progressive democracy in Japan will have to reckon with for decades to come. Who can fail to regret that troublesome forces have been stored up by processes that could have been avoided without crossing in the slightest the natural desire of the American government to preserve the integrity of American society and the standards of American labor?

Still, as the good mariner always tries to take his reckonings, no matter how dim the stars, so I am under obligations to bring into the record all the outstanding facts which promise to help us in attaining the

great object of unbroken peace between two countries
that have nothing on earth to gain by an armed conflict over any subject whatsoever. I refer to the peoples of the two countries, not to individual political
merchants who supply munitions of war or ambitious
concession-seekers who may make fortunes in Mon-
golia, Manchuria, and Siberia. Now first among the
outstanding facts in the present situation, is the un-
precedented industrial progress of Japan since 1914 —
industrial progress which inevitably makes her the
formidable competitor with the other mercantile nations of the West in exploiting the mainland of Asia. It
is likely that the competition will become keener and
keener and that diplomatic incidents connected with
the fight for markets will come thicker and faster.
This means that Japan and America will have more
knotty problems to solve in the future than in the old
days when Japan had nothing but raw materials to
sell and was a customer, not a competitor. It is in-
conceivable that any one of these problems will be
worth a harsh word, but in international affairs it frequently happens that the real cause of a dispute is
utterly unknown to the majority who quarrel violently
about some supposed issue. Every sentiment that in-
terferes with the settlement of future controversies
on their merits hampers the maintenance of cordial relations, is an undesirable impediment in the way of
" getting down to brass tacks " in discussing commercial disputes. While the fortunes of Russia and China
remain unsettled and their place in the world remains
anomalous, the issues arising between Japan and America will be all the more perplexing, and their happy

solution will require unclouded minds and a high re-
solve to allow no controversy to verge into an angry
quarrel.

The second outstanding element in the present situation is the fact, if I may venture to be bold, that Japan
will be a potent force in the destinies of the Orient,
because she has capital, an industrial establishment,
an army, and a navy. Are not these the outward
signs of sovereignty that command respect in the councils of the West? At all events they seem to have
weight in the councils of the East. For a long time,
there has been growing up in certain circles in Japan
a philosophy of politics that would give Japan supremacy in Oriental affairs similar to that enjoyed by
the United States in this hemisphere. I do not say
that this philosophy is right, but merely that it exists;
and I am somewhat puzzled by its reception. May I
ask what is the moral difference between the policy
of America in extending her dominion over the Carib-
bean and in protecting her capitalists in their Latin-
American investments, and the policy of Japan in
widening her sphere of empire in Asia and supporting
her capitalists in their forward-looking enterprises?
To my Oriental mind, there seems to be no moral difference, but that may be due to my lack of acute penetration. Whatever the answer to this particular question, there remains an alternative policy — a policy
sanctioned by enlightened liberalism, namely the policy
of coöperation with one's neighbors rather than acquisition and dominance. In any event, Japan will have
undoubted influence in all the affairs of the Pacific; and
by virtue of that fact, in all the conflicts and adjust-

ments arising among the powers now operating in that sphere. Japan therefore will be a factor to be reckoned with in shifting balances of power, and all the periodical re-settlements of the European estate.

Here I take leave of this delicate subject. There is a large and powerful party in Japan that confidently expects the United States to challenge Japan's economic advance on the mainland of Asia, and looks upon every measure directed against Japanese in America and possible immigrants as an evidence of enmity toward the Japanese nation. What America will ultimately do in the prosecution of her economic interests in Asia, I do not pretend to know. I confess to the belief that America's actions with reference to immigrants and migration are not framed in a spirit of hostility to the Japanese nation. I say this in spite of the bitter anti-Japanese utterances to be found in certain newspapers, periodicals, and political orations. But is it strange that the methods pursued by the Congress of the United States in passing the exclusion bill should convince thousands of Japanese people that America has no confidence in the Japanese government, in its pledges and its integrity, and cares not a fig for its friendship or coöperation? I repeat, is it strange, especially in view of the fact that immigration was not in reality an issue in the case, — above all in view of the fact that the one and only issue was whether a controversy which had hitherto been dealt with in friendly coöperation — a controversy on which we already had an amicable agreement — should find its ultimate solution at a council table or be bluntly and inexorably disposed of by one of the parties to the old understanding? Let us admit, for the sake of argument, that Japan has not the slightest claim upon the consideration of Congress; let us admit that it was a mistake for President Roosevelt ever to enter into the Gentlemen's Agreement. The first fact remains, and it had sunk deeply into the consciousness of the Japanese people, that the vexatious issue was one that had once been adjusted in friendly coöperation and that could always be handled in the same spirit and in the same way; I repeat, for the wrong impression prevails in many quarters in America, the issue was not immigration. As far as affording any outlet for the peasants and laborers of Japan is concerned that issue was closed years ago, and any additional guarantees required for the security of American national life would have been gladly yielded. The sole issue was the method of handling an affair on which a friendly agreement already existed. To my Oriental mind the procedure of Congress is inexplicable. But my personal opinion is unimportant. The grave consequences flow from the fact that it is now very difficult for any Japanese liberal to convince the conservatives and the nationalists that the process by which the immigration bill was passed was not intended to serve notice on Japan that she need expect no more coöperation from America, and that the ruthless pursuit of national interests without respect for the feelings of others is not a high and noble quality of patriotism. In saying this I am uttering no criticism of America. The grave consequences to which I refer will affect the social development of Japan far more than the destiny of America.

As I have recorded in my previous lectures, there was growing up in Japan a liberalism that made for domestic reform and international coöperation. The conditions of Japanese life made it difficult for that force to flourish, but it has been making remarkable gains in recent years. Those who gave their lives and risked their fortunes in that cause cherished a vision of a fortunate union of Western and Oriental values.

The East and West had lived together and developed together from the dawn of history until the rise of the Saracens cut the world in two; and then the twain were forced to follow lonely paths separately. The nineteenth century opened a new era in bringing the East and West back again to a common ground of prosperity and fraternity. When the "Black Ships" of America lay at anchor at Uraga in 1846, Japan little dreamed what a new rôle was soon to be given to her. Nor did America realize what destiny had in store for her. It was the meeting of the East and West after the separation of a thousand years. Without making any immodest boast, I may be permitted to say that Japan, because of her unbroken peace of three long centuries, was preserving and developing the essence of the Oriental civilization — Buddhism, Confucianism, Literature, Medicine, Mathematics, Arts, and Political Institutions. The precious heritage of thousands of generations in India and China was kept in sacred custody in Japan.

When the gates were once opened, the new civilization of the West now rushed into Japan like an avalanche. From one end of the Empire to the other, Japanese minds were astir. Since the introduction of

Buddhism in the Sixth Century, the Japanese had never been so profoundly moved. They looked across the ocean and saw the great Republic of America, young and vigorous with new blood and new life. The civilization of Europe in all its different shades was converging on her, for America was certainly the melting pot of the Western culture and achievement.

Would the meeting of America and Japan open a new page in the progress of mankind? The hope ran high in Japanese minds. Sensitive and proud, the Japanese nation set her mind on the new rôle of amalgamating the two civilizations. She introduced steam engines, telephones, the parliamentary system, laboratories, and armaments. The occidentalization of Japan was fast taking place. Who can blame Japan for imitating the West? Is there any categorical difference between originality and imitation? Was not the great social heritage of mankind made possible by imitation among humanity?

In fifty years Japan won three international wars and secured her political integrity. She revised her treaties with the Western powers and won back judicial independence and her right to control her own tariffs. She was admitted to the family of nations, and she felt that she was given a recognition as a sister and an equal.

When the national calamity of September 1, 1923 smote her down, the heart of the whole world reached out to Japan in sublime sympathy and gallant rescue. The American nation arose as one person and rushed to Japan with material and moral help. The heart of

Japan was touched to the core. The emotion was too deep for words or tears.

The American Ambassador, Mr. Cyrus E. Woods, was idolized, as a symbol of Japanese gratitude. When he was leaving Japan two months after the disaster, he was called upon by a Japanese, a stranger and apparently a man of no great means. This aged man approached the Ambassador and, taking out of a paper a set of Japanese kimono, said, "My dear Ambassador, I am a poor citizen of Tokyo. My house was burned and I lost everything. At the time of despair, I read in the paper that your great country was coming to our rescue with such a generosity and sympathy. It went a thousand miles deep into my heart. I heard that you were returning home. I have nothing and I have no capacity whatsoever to express my gratitude to your great people. I remembered, however, that I had one thing left uninjured by the fire. It is this kimono. I take this to you in order to thank you and your nation by giving up the last of my earthly possessions." It moved the kind-hearted Ambassador. He could not speak. Tears stood in both men's eyes. The hearts of the two nations thus beat as one. Cynics may call it sentimental. But sentiments very often carry farther than material interest.

It is no wonder that the Japanese, particularly the old Japanese, are keeping America dear to their hearts. Brought up in the tradition of friendship and good will, they learned to respect and love America. Emerson, Washington and Lincoln were household words in our country. The manifestation of sympathy after the earthquake was a climax of affection.

Then came the Immigration Act of 1924 so suddenly. It was such an abrupt change that the Japanese could not at first grasp the meaning. It was unexpected and it was incomprehensible. It seemed to some Japanese as though we were told that our place was not in the company of the world powers, and that all our past endeavors were thrown to the winds. Old Japan, however, stood unshaken in her confidence in American good will; but are you surprised, that young Japan lost its patience if not its faith? Young Japan was brought up in the new competitive age when the relationship of our two nations was not exactly the same as in the early years of the restoration. The Immigration Act naturally worked in no beneficial way. Here I think the great cause for future concern lies. Old Japan is the ruler of the present, but Young Japan is the ruler of the future.

Just before I left Japan, a noted writer of Tokyo came out in a strong article, saying: " Japan, turn your face to Asia. You have turned your back to Asia too long. It is in Asia that you will be warmly received as a friend." Sympathetic friends will not fail to read in these lines a pathetic note of disappointment running through the appeal.

We never thought the greatness of real America lay in her material wealth or physical strength. There were many rich and powerful countries in ancient times; but they are all gone. They were as transitory as the great clouds that traverse their sepulchres. As permanent greatness is seen only in the sublimity of spirit and manifest in enduring forms of beauty and power, Japan's ambition has always been to attain a

height of spiritual serenity. Japan looked and still looks
to America as the torch-bearer of Western civilization
— the emancipation of humanity and brotherhood of
man. Will Japan's hope be fulfilled? With wistful-
ness and yearning Japan is watching the future de-
velopments in American politics. We have not lost
our faith. We are awaiting with breathless interest, the
manifestation of American spirit, the traditional spirit
of fair play and serene justice.

COLUMBIA UNIVERSITY PRESS
COLUMBIA UNIVERSITY
NEW YORK

FOREIGN AGENT
HUMPHREY MILFORD
AMEN HOUSE, E.C.
LONDON